ON PATRICK WHITE'S DILEMMAS

Vrasidas Karalis

ON PATRICK WHITE'S DILEMMAS

A Personal Essay

Vrasidas Karalis

Brandl & Schlesinger

First published by Brandl & Schlesinger in 2025
PO Box 127 Blackheath NSW 2785 Australia
www.brandl.com.au

ISBN 978-0-6452350-7-4 (print)
ISBN 978-0-6452350-8-1 (epdf)
ISBN 978-0-6452350-9-8 (epub)

A catalogue record for this book is available from the National Library of Australia

Cover and book design by Andras Berkes-Brandl

Printed by Pegasus Print

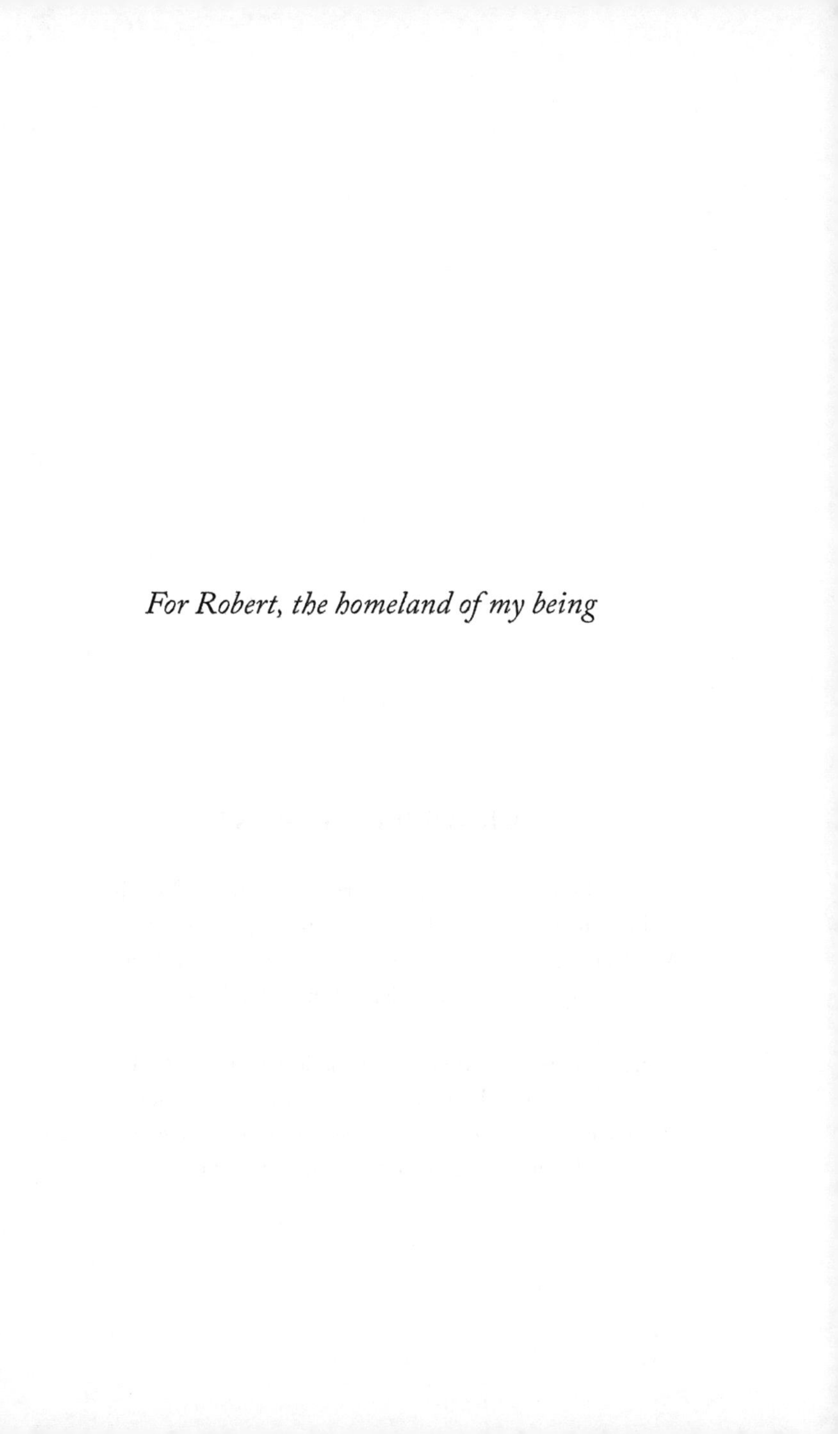

For Robert, the homeland of my being

ACKNOWLEDGEMENTS

I would like to thank Katia Ariel and Adrian Martin for the editing of the text in different stages of its writing. My gratitude to Veronica and Andras who as independent publishers still release unsellable books.

The book is dedicated to the shadow of Robert Meader.
We read all Patrick White's novels together
and haven't forgotten the expression on his face every time
he encountered something amaaazing…

Patrick White saved words from oblivion.
Manoly Lascaris

The Accidental Searches for You

Nowadays, Patrick White's novels are read by accident. No one recommends them. Almost no university courses include any of his works. "They are unusable in our cultural wars," an academic friend said. Another one added: "They can never become films." I searched persistently for an opportunity to explore the world of the unusable, unfilmable novelist, Patrick White. To this day, I don't know why.

Perhaps, because of our first encounter. I remember it vaguely. It must have been around

1976 or 77. I was still at high school. Greece had her perennial political problems: dictatorships, economic crises, political instability – the usual folklore of societies resisting modernity. My personal circumstances must have contributed, too. Until I turned fourteen, I was an albino. Totally colourless, white hair, bleached skin, with blue eyes – really odd. All olive-skinned, black-hair, dark-eyed Mediterraneans poked serious fun at me. I rubbed ink on my face to look darker and avoid the daily ridicule.

I had to make the most of it, of course. I skipped school, wandered around the woods along the banks of the sacred river Alpheus, and conversed frantically with the spirits of the past. Oftentimes, I found refuge with my grandmother who, illiterate as she was, wanted me to know, from newspapers and magazines, the news from around the world. It was a ritual we had established several years earlier. She told me legends about the past. "Stories about the old Greeks, the giants, back then." In exchange, I read to her "things about today or yesterday people."

At a strange bookshop, in the provincial town of Pyrgos which was selling just about everything I found a huge, 650-page long volume entitled *The Tree of Man* (1955). It was printed on thick, heavy paper. I struggled to open its pages with a paper-cutter. "It's about Australia, grandma," I said.

Half of our village migrated to Melbourne in the early 1960s. I was an infant, but I still have some misty recollections of men and women dancing, singing and eating at common meals in the village square days before their departure, farewelling their native land, repeating the arcane word *Afstralia, Afstralia*. Where are we going? Who knows when we will see each other again? Children said that to their parents, and friends to friends. They were going to the richest country in the world, the earthly paradise of abundance and wealth.

My grandmother was curious to know how those blissful people lived in *Afstralia*. "Do they ever get tired of harvesting dollars from the money-tree?" she wondered. "They must be really rich, unlike us who live in misery," she sighed.

I started reading the first paragraphs and carried on for three or four pages. *The man was a young man. Life had not yet operated on his face.* She turned restless and fidgety. "Operated on his face?" she wondered. I continued: *The name of this man was Stan Parker. While he was still unborn his mother had thought she would like to call him Ebenezer...* She stopped me. "Ebenezer? What sort of name is that?"

I kept reading when, some 30 minutes later, she erupted: "*Afstralia* is much worse than here. Only poverty, and bad luck. All is dry there. Strange names, too. Why did so many of us go there? Anyway, nothing happens in this story!" She exclaimed in utter frustration: "Can you read me from the *Story of Alexander the Great*? At least he was walking and talked with many exotic creatures." I left the huge volume aside, and never finished it. But never forgot the syncopated syntax: *The cart stopped, grazing the hairy side of a tree, and the horse, shaggy and stolid as the tree, sighed and took root.*

Years later, in Athens, I met one of the translators. "Don't remind me," he cried in despair, "of that dreadful flop. There was something deeply awkward in that novel. I couldn't get into its rhythm. I couldn't crack its language or the tone of the writer's voice. We split it in half with somebody else, and our different approaches can be felt. But the style was so awkward, so clumsy, so un-English. I studied at Oxford, you know. That was not the real English I was used to. The glorious English of E.M. Foster, Evelyn Waugh and Graham Greene. But this…? This was English minus its glamour. Colloquial, demotic, peripheral, yet baroque and inflated. Paradoxical, is it not? It was beyond me. But I had to do it for money and the publicity after the Nobel Prize." He talked fast and ceaselessly. Never met him again.

Meanwhile, some months later, on the island of Santorini, I met Cassandra, an Australian girl from Brisbane, in love with a local wine producer. She gave me a book called *A Love of Swann*. Long sentences, she added. I cannot follow them. It was early September in the year of the Lord Nineteen Eighty, when I was seduced by Marcel Proust. No Patrick White. No Australia. Only Proust for the best years of my youth. And all because of an Australian girl from Brisbane named Cassandra.

Getting to know each other again

Strange *non sequiturs* happen in life. In 1988, I found myself stranded in Amsterdam. Abandoned, confused and sad. The weather was wet, foggy and miserable. I was fading out. I was in a bad state. Flirting with depression. Frantically, I rummaged through the bookshops around the Centrum struggling for anything that would keep my curiosity alive, my mind sane and my good taste sharp.

The Atheneum Bookshop in Spuistraat had heaps of remainders. Mostly, American Viking editions, with rough edges, heavy hardcovers in dazzling dustjackets. And at startling prices. Ten guilders for big books like James Joyce's *Ulysses,* Bruce Chatwin's *The Songlines*, Sergei Eisenstein's *Immoral Memories*, Leo Tolstoy's *War and Peace*, even the King James Bible in a beautifully gilded edition. Together with Hemingway, Scott Fitzgerald,

Thomas Wolfe, Flannery O'Connor, V.S. Naipul, Milan Kundera, and the exotic flavours of the time: Gabriel García Márquez, Julio Cortázar, Jorge Luis Borges and Carlos Fuentes. All cheap and charming and unread. There and then, in the remainders section, in an existential impasse, in the freezing cold of the European north, I re-entered Patrick White's world, and a life-long romance began. I was twenty-eight by then. The need for strong bonds was invincible – and my time for adventures and experiments was up.

In the beginning, I found his later books, *Memoirs of Many in One* (1986) and *The Eye of the Storm* (1973). Certainly, not the best introduction to his work. The first was too self-referential, the second too self-conscious. In the former, White unleashed his drollness and, in the latter, affectionately mocked his own respectability. For *Memoirs,* he garnered mostly negative reviews. For *The Eye of the Storm,* he was awarded the Nobel Prize. Everything differs here: the scope of the story, the tonal vibrations in language, the abrupt and Shakespearean transitions from the sublime to the ridiculous and vice versa, the horribly enchanting and wonderfully unlovable characters. I felt compelled to keep searching for more.

I spent my hapless youth stooping over the pages of Cervantes, Lawrence Sterne, Gustave Flaubert, Émile Zola, Guy de Maupassant, Gogol, Turgenev, Leo Tolstoy, Aleksandr Solzhenitsyn, Fyodor Dostoevsky, Thomas Mann, Marguerite Yourcenar, Murasaki Shikibu, Yukio Mishima, Tahar Ben Jellun, Naguib Mahfouz, Alexandros Papadiamandis, Georgios Vizyinos, Yiorgos Theotokas and Nikos Kazantzakis. Did I mention Marcel Proust? Two full years, two hot summers in the Greek islands, reading only Proust in Greek and French. And the poets? How can I forget that all my youthful *élan vital* was devoured by T.S Eliot? And Rilke and Valery and Cavafy? All exacerbated by that ghastly place, the University of Athens, which killed my imagination unto these concluding days of my existence. What was wrong with me? I felt old already at twenty-eight. Why? I wondered about this in rare moments of transcendental illumination.

Because of such existential stupefaction, I could appreciate ambition, empathise with difference, even understand failure. But in White, there was an uncanny tone of voice, with a strange sonority in its words and confusing music in its sentences. It was like a reminder, like a message, like an imperceptible nod by some "impalpable impressions on the air" that were hovering over me. I still remember talking incoherently with myself: "Too much music in these books, relentless music. Both symphonic and chamber. Mahler, perhaps? German romantics? Brahms or List? And what about his displaced romanticism? And his antimodernist modernism? His exploration of veiled human kindness, even if his characters dislike their own self or their own goodness? *For I do not that good which I will; but the evil which I hate, that I do.* In the end, everything turns out so Biblical – doesn't it?

In Holland, I was commuting daily on the most punctual railways in the world. Sitting quietly on impeccably clean seats, I could enjoy White's buzzy and fuzzy prose while being surrounded by cautious and respectful commuters: and yes, yes, I was reading literature for the sheer pleasure of it, for the purity of reading, and the enjoyment of language, not out of any professional obligation or civic duty. I didn't intend to write reviews, exhibit my critical acumen or indulge in the mystifications of academic jargon to secure my position as avant-garde or my status as a radical academic.

This is what honest readers can do: engage dialogically with texts. Become one with the characters without reducing them to autobiographical notes, ideological obsessions or narcissistic projections. *To see them as differential variations of an all-encompassing theme and not as a series of studies of what looks like me.* Only such a differentiating reading can save texts from silence and irrelevance by foregrounding their architectural plan and the overarching theme that made it imaginable and ultimately written. This can save readers from the blasphemy of omniscience, of the hollow posturing that they control the text, of explaining what needs no explanation. Always differentiate, never take over, never project. We must read texts as spaces of variation, of positive alienation and othering – from us. Anyhow. Vras, stop talking to yourself. Patrick White wrote that Greeks are speech-mad, and there you go. Confirming the stereotype is no good.

The long trip from Amsterdam to Maastricht was smooth and uneventful. We cannot really understand our response to a book without reconstructing the conditions around us when we first read it. Understanding implies the evocation of the actual experience of its *first* reading: where, when, with whom (or without whom). The act of reading revives the invisible thread, the emotional recall, that weaves the continuity between past and present, and therefore establishes patterns of self-recognition. Art forms link human minds: making them converge through the ultimate code of disclosure, language.

The written word came out of White's pages like a living voice, loud and clear; it was distinct, dense and pulsating – even for a non-native. I forgot where I was. Reading relocated me. Reading abolished time. *Reaching up, her arms were rounded by increasing light. In the street an early worker stared as he passed but looked away on recognising a ceremony.* Where am I? In Shakespeare-land? I asked myself this after the last page of *The Eye of the Storm.*

Yes, I, the reader, witnessed an unexpected ceremony, a rite of passage to the unveiling of the known. I was part of it, I was at the heart of a ritual. *The light she could not ward off: it was by now too solid, too possessive; herself possessed.* There you go: possessed at last. That was the word. Absorbed by a world I knew nothing about: a new continent, the new country of the mind, its fragmented syntax exploring meanings unknown to me. Possessed and grateful. And exhausted. The world expanded. Short sentences, brief snapshots, verbal polychromy. It was excessive. And seductive. It was abundant. It was exhaustive, indeed.

Soon, I discovered his other books. I read *Flaws in The Glass* (1981) at least four times within the same month. So many references to Greek history in there. All taste wrong, of course, and all are full of love. He had misunderstood so many things about the Motherland. Everything was blown out of proportion by his naïve, rudderless liberalism searching for melodramas of rebellion and epics of resistance in one of the most conformist and amorphous societies on the shores of the Middle Sea. "How did he get it so wrong?" I asked myself.

White, of course, wrote about his 'other country' through somebody else's eyes. And, as a suspicious reader, I could see the eyes and the tears, the love and the repulsion, I could recognise the sarcasm and the disappointment, the irony toward his own vain hope to imagine that he had found a second country, where the first one had already caused him so much trouble and loved her dearly for this. *You Greeks*, he wrote in 1982, *gave the world civilisation. Since the fall of Byzantium it has been preserved by the Panayia and the Saints – as you know in your hearts, even those of you who profess not to 'believe'.* I can't help but smile at the passionate rhetoric of such romantic Utopians. But they are the usual misunderstandings of ardent love and blind passion. Virgin Mary, Orthodox saints,

Turkish Occupation, Marx, Lenin, and the socialist leader of the 1980s, Andreas Papandreou: that was a scary potpourri of curiosities, a mausoleum of horrors, destined to have quite an unhappy ending – as it did, several years later.

Mr Manoly Lascaris looms large in the background of these statements: he himself was that imaginary Hellas, the eternal homeland, his personal *longue durée,* the ideal refuge inhabited by brave freedom fighters, medieval heroic defenders at the borders and uncompromised idealists ready to sacrifice themselves for any cause imaginable. He, Mr Lascaris, the aristocrat, the presumed heir to an imperial dynasty of Byzantium, the high-minded snob, the dreaming expatriate. There was no contradiction there – but it is too early to bring him into this discussion.

What makes his self-portrait unique and enduring is what himself describes as *a very strong sense of vulgarity*. It infuses the narrative with pulsating earthiness and passionate corporeality, energised by a disturbing sense of sincerity and honesty. In an era of auto-fictionalisation, *Flaws in the Glass* challenges pretensions and confabulations. White's intention is simple and devastating: *any literary reputation that can't stand up to the truth isn't worth having*. The truth, ah the truth. And what is the truth? as Pontius Pilate asked. But that's an entirely different conversation.

Something personal

As a reader, I always try to go through a writer's complete oeuvre – and do it backwards. First, their last book, and then all the way to the beginning. For some writers, like Ernest Hemingway, their first book is their best. Hemingway never went beyond the stylistic acrobatics of *In Our Time* (1925) or indeed certain paragraphs of *A Farewell to Arms* (1929). His later books are hypochondriac, shallow and sentimental: more Eugene Sue and Maria Corelli than Hemingway.

The same can be said about F. Scott Fitzgerald, and of course the rambunctious Thomas Wolfe, the bitter ironist Saul Bellow or the supercilious David Foster Wallace. For many, their last books reveal what they tried to do or, more precisely, who they try to be all their life. Toward the end, they simplify their diction, abandon pretence, drop all inessential enthusiasms, denude themselves of all desire to impress or boast or flatter or hallucinate. They refrain from making pronouncements and revert to confessions, or struggle again and again to compose before the end, "the only true book which already exists in each one of us," according to Proust.

Being toward the end, they can only write about the primacy of their *enfleshed presence* (as Les Murray called it): their swan song is the most appealing, direct, unaffected, most sincere revelation about their ailing and aging body, while their mind is still at its sharpest and most vulnerable state, when all resistance to reality is suspended. Proust's monastic eroticism is the most interesting example, as he changed the particulars of Bergotte's death after himself having gone through a near-death experience. Another example, Jean-Paul Sartre's *The Words* (1963): simple, personal, unpretentious – to the degree that Sartre could ever be unpretentious. Or Nikos Kazantzakis' *Report to*

Greco (1957): serene, Homeric, unclouded. Or Vladimir Nabokov's *Speak, Memory* (1951): transparent, cinematic, tempered. Or Naguib Mahfouz's *Echoes of an Autobiography* (1994): oneiric, photographic, evocative.

Having abandoned the usual annoying exuberance of their self-confidence, and the fatal fascination with plot (so lethally celebrated by E.M. Foster in his imperial Anglosphere or Martin Amis in his post-imperial melancholia), they talk about what really matters to them, and yet have no command over its articulation. Their movements through history, the unfolding of their consciousness over time, and, most alarmingly, the story of coming to terms with their corporeal presence and its decline. They affectionately confront their own personal or private myths, strip them naked, and greet them farewell. They know that they were innocent and debilitating illusions but now, just before the final night, they *are* the writer's life, indeed the centre of an existence.

In the end, nothing matters more than the only paradise we all ever know, the fragile and crumbling home of our uniqueness and suffering, our brittle and frail body. And how we feel in that body, how others look at us, and how we love and hate it simultaneously – and how it betrays us slyly and mercilessly. A similar trajectory guided me through White's work. *The Twyborn Affair* (1979) and *The Solid Mandala* (1966) followed by *Riders in the Chariot* (1961) – all of them about the adventures of the human body, the invisible protagonist of all White's universe.

As predestined by the great architect of coincidences, one day, I was walking along Amsterdam's Prinsengracht when, in front of me, there was a pile of books on the footpath with a piece of paper declaring: *Engelse Boeken Gratis.* Under the enormous paperbacks by Wilbur Smith, Barbara Cartland and Stephen King, there they stood: *The Vivisector* (1970), *Voss* (1957) and *The Tree of Man* – all in hardcover, American editions, unread and pristine, with their cryptic dustjackets intact.

I opened one of them, I can't remember which. The mustiness of its pages brought back the Queen of my reading life, my illiterate grandmother. The humid room where we tried to read White for the first time, the fireplace, the fresh bread, the unforgettable rainy day, and her, my Thetis, archetypal and Platonic, smelling of lavender and coffee. Such involuntary memories enhanced the epiphany of reading. They immersed me in the unsettling awe we experience when we encounter something greater than us. It must have been *Voss*, then.

I read all three books in five days, and still recall the excitement. I could have written these myself, had I been born in a better country and in brighter times. But the 1980s were the 80s and I still try to forget them – but who can ever forget the delusions and the transgressions of their misguided youth? Everything we believed was wrong and uplifting. These books truly hit me head on. I felt elated and annoyed. They showed me how simplistic, irrelevant and parochial I was.

Oh, no... I am going to Australia

Then, the accident of accidents happened, the most unexpected of things. Holland was too cold, too elusive, and too Dutch. Since day two of my arrival, I was applying for jobs everywhere, from Kathmandu to Santiago, from Helsinki to Johannesburg. And it happened. Out of the blue, three years later, I was offered a lectureship at the University of Sydney. It was pure accident. One cold morning, around 7.30, the wintery month of June down under, I landed in White's country. After having trotted around the planet from Patagonia to Siberia and from Iceland to India, I thought that it was the right time to become a tree and grow roots in my late 20s. The wanderer domesticated and homed. Time to settle down and feel at ease in the world. I became the first paragraph of *The Tree of Man*.

It was June of 1991, Paul Keating was still the Treasurer, Australia was in the recession that "we had to have", and Patrick White was dead for over a year. The opportunity to read his books surrounded by the sounds of the speech that gave them existence was almost ironic. Beyond all academic indulgence for self-dramatization, I have a special gift for listening. Being an outsider, I undertook as my moral duty to listen how the native tongue was spoken, absorb its rhythms, decode its metaphors, relive its poetic truths, elope into its imaginary landscapes and ultimately enjoy its daily prose.

In brief, I love listening to people talking about themselves. And I love keeping notes of their incoherent rants. It is the changing pitch in their voice that I struggle to capture, the *vernacular orality* distinct and ungraspable in each language, full of non-sequiturs, grammatical errors and syntactic irregularities. However, I had to remain someone who *foreignises* their language, retaining the undomesticated and un-assimilated diverting tropes of another language, in collusion or collision.

More than anything else, I love listening to people talking *to themselves*, as most people always do, even if they pretend to discuss. I remained phonocentric more than logocentric, as a modern Sophist defined it. In other words, more Socrates than Gorgias, with deep suspicion but immense devotion to the act of writing. Faith comes through listening, as someone said, although we remain faithful through writing.

From my early days in Sydney, I was fascinated by the uncanonical and fluid structure of speaking, especially for the strong currents of orality that define everyday speech in Australia, a country which found its Shakespeare in the cadences of television news readers. The British perform a language of rules; the Australians act out a language of singularities. The accent, the intonation, the tempo, the rhythmic patterns are distinct, anarchic, uncanonical, a mixture of background idiolects and the canonical dialect in constant hybridisation. And for all those who learn English as their second language, the positioning of verbs, adverbs and conjunctives in a sentence is proof of this. In a secular world without sacred books, the greatest and ultimate Bible is the human mouth.

When a Lebanese friend told me: "Good you are not but," my mind went immediately to the famous opening paragraph of *Voss*: *There is a man, miss, asking for your uncle, said Rose. And stood breathing. What man? Asked the young woman....* You feel that there is something uncanny here, but you cannot define it. Or in *The Solid Mandala*: *Mrs*

Poulter manoeuvred past the fuchsias. To ring the police. At least she could thank her friend for reminding her of the obvious, though even so, she was not so very grateful. For the moment her leg was hurting more than her thoughts. The rain didn't exactly wet, but warned, out of the purple – looking clouds. The light had deepened until it was sort of moss-coloured. You must re-read the passage to capture its rhythm. There is something Joycean in this plus a sense of drollness. Like at the final sentence of the same novel: *Then she turned, to do the expected things, before re-entering her actual sphere of life.* White uses quirky structures so that the actual sphere of life turns imaginary. His syntax transforms the narration into a commentary of the narrative.

Many wacky expressions from the play *A Cheery Soul* (1963) also popped up: *Sometimes I think those blessed tomatoes will block the light completely*. Or: *Everyone'll tell you I'm the cheerfulest person. Normally. But there are moments in life which aren't normal … when you are dislocated so to speak.* The language of his plays is full of the most awkward, most eccentric expressions which are excellent performative tools to visualise personal idiosyncrasies. *Waddayaknow* is enough to reveal the character, but it would only be a quip if it was not followed by shattering realisations: *We must be stronger than our bodies ... even when we imagine the spirit has abandoned us.*

White knows how to crack witty jokes, as is almost compulsory in Australia, but always goes a step further and translates them into the terms and conditions of tragedy. He feels that behind a smiling face there is an unrecognised adventure full of anxieties, failures and phobias. In his emblematically perverse way, White says something flippant when we expect a profundity, and a profundity when we expect a joke. *Personally,* as Miss Docker would say, *I like a good discussion, amongst friends, on a metaphysical theme.*

And I still wonder: is this a joke or not?

On White's Dilemmas

In an era when all grand narratives are deconstructed and only individual stories exist, can a discussion between friends revolve around a metaphysical theme? White's strange statement framed my own dilemma, the dilemma of all our contemporaries lost in the confusion caused by the mechanical repetition of sellable and disposable ideas through social media, promotion mechanisms and academic jargon.

I grew up with the sculptural prose of Marguerite Yourcenar's *Memoirs of Hadrian* (1951), Hermann Broch's serpentine psychology in *The Death of Virgil* (1945), and Leo Tolstoy's chronicles of self-memorialisation in *War and Peace* (1869) – languages complete in themselves, which truly shatter the certainties of their readers. They exhibit a marked circularity, a classical self-sufficiency that indicates a solid and centred subjectivity. From the beginning you understand where they are coming from and where they want to take you. And you go along. They have chosen the way for you.

It was impossible to feel the same with White. First of all, within the context of our cultural wars today, he is so out of synch, as they say. You read someone who does not celebrate any form of victimhood, any ideal Utopia or indeed any "pristine positionality" of the self. He is one of the last writers for whom writing is part of their self-unfolding process, not the core of their self-definition. You understand that his writings posit questions that go beyond their actual subject matter. His characters never really identify with their actions. The end of his novels leaves everything in an uneasy resignation. Nothing is resolved, no one is absolved. No catharsis because the drama now lives in the mind of the reader. You also sense that there are many invisible texts within his texts which, despite remaining unarticulated, come through forcefully. *But Judd had lived beyond grief. He was impressed, rather, by the great simplicity with which everything had happened.*

For each character, a separate novel could be written; each episode is a distinct story with its subplots; every chapter is a short novella that can stand alone as independent reading. His writing is about articulating the multiplicities that confuse us. The writer does not victimise himself; he doesn't feel wounded. He doesn't suffer from the "creative illness" that psychoanalysis has told us about. The naturalness of human dysfunctionality is truly impressive: no explanation is needed, or justification provided. This is how things are – and how humans interact. The rest is literature and cannot be recorded.

I was particularly overwhelmed by *The Vivisector* and *Voss*, with their reluctance to draw conclusions about their very subject matter, using irony, self-irony mostly, to highlight the self-declared inability of the novel to fulfil the expectations that the writer himself sets for his writing. There can be no unity of subject-matter, as there is no unity of style. In *Riders in the Chariot* and *The Twyborn Affair*, style becomes part of the story. The relaxed and somehow self-conscious prose of the *Vivisector* is also part of the story's unfolding. White writes as if he doesn't really know what is happening in his narratives, or indeed in his own mind. He composes grand statements which parody themselves because of their absolute truthfulness: *In the headmistress's wooden words, he could hear the stubborn music that was waiting for release. Of rock and scrub. Of winds curled invisible in wombs of air. Of thin rivers struggling towards seas of eternity. All flowing and uniting. Over a bed of upturned faces.* In Voss's final chapter, we encounter the climactic consummation of Proust's aesthetic radicalism, the ultimate fruition of the novel's capacity to articulate what they use to call 'the theatre of memory.'

Initially, we feel bemused by the deliberate and obvious parody of his own style, full of acerbic wit and mischievous self-mockery. Parodying yourself is an achievement of the highest rank: very few writers, after Cervantes or Lawrence Stern, have managed to be themselves and beyond themselves simultaneously. In a sense, herein the difference is found between an *écrivain* and an *écrivant*, so aptly delineated by that desperado *logomythologist*, Roland Barthes, with language being a battlefield and language being a mirror.

White could never find peace within language. Like every *écrivain*, he was tormented by his own struggle to find a linguistic self, an identifiable verbal space, in which his existence would locate its centre and also illustrate its ex-centricity. But, as a paradoxical *écrivant*, he wanted to record the reflection of each moment as a small pebble of an endless mosaic. The *écrivain* was toying with conceptual signifiers, the *écrivant* was enthralled by the signified. He lived in both realms at the same time; but he could not choose, and he was unable to surrender to either. His oscillation illustrates his dilemmas as a writer.

The scope and the variety of his prosopographies were truly overwhelming. His aesthetic curiosity and intellectual voraciousness frame his constant effort not to disregard any possible form of life or pattern of behaviour. Like a committed naturalist who wants to record, describe and name all creatures great and small, White struggles to foreground and pinpoint all forms of being and doing. I call his works *novels of expansion*: his narrative never ends, being itself the *roman fleuve* that explores its unreachable horizons.

Unlike, however, Romain Rolland, whose *Jean Christophe* (1904-1912) was the template for many novels that formed White's youth and can be sensed somewhere in the background of *The Vivisector*, White focuses not on the idealised ideotypes of the stories but on the creative defects that deepen sensitivity and awareness about what is narrated. His characters are always at a dead-end; they confront their own limitations which they cannot surpass or deepen. Unlike, similarly, the popular ideas of Somerset W. Maugham as displayed in *The Razor's Edge* (1944), no philosophy can be revealed in India or elsewhere. The essence of being is unveiled here and now, amongst trivialities and restrictions, without concepts or ideas, but as unconscious acts and unintended deeds. *Voss did not die, Miss Trevelyan replied. He is still there, it is said, in the country, and always will be. His legend will be written down, eventually, by those who have been troubled by it.* His characters reveal who they are when least expected. From his first novel to the last, the cardinal question 'who is the narrator?' takes unexpected connotations. White presents a fundamental disagreement between the narrative and the narrator: he turns the one against the other.

Such a dichotomy impresses from the very first reading: how can we trust language to frame the experience of a reality that resists articulation? But this dilemma gives us the key to unlock the possibilities of style itself, and the personality inherent in that style. *Yphos* (style) is *ethos*, the ancients used to say. Or *Le style est l'homme même*, according to Comte de Buffon. Yes and no: we must learn to live with such ambiguous answers. Style is not always the individual. In the era marked by the immersive illusions of journalistic realism, White's prose presents something uniquely anachronistic, distancing and liberating.

His prose makes the claim that the novel's structure points to something beyond the novelist, something that touches upon the fears and fancies of readers at the very moment they feel lost and horizonless, surrounded by commodities they don't need, machines that manipulate them and luxuries that distract them from exploring the thick darkness of their mind that yearns for grace or self-destruction. In brief, today's readers want to find everywhere projections of themselves or representations of their tribal customs. Hence, they become terribly disappointed by the affectionate mockery that they find in White's works of all their popular shibboleths, even of art or God, class or gender, together with all other dissimulations of so-called lived experience.

Yet we all know that literature is about *unlived* experiences; it represents what we can only live through means of literature, and never imagined possible before. What Voss finds in the country of the mind he is lost in is the impossible, what was thought unachievable, but was always in front of us. And that is also what we find in White's best works.

White thrives on digressions: he never misses the chance to say something enigmatic and leave it incomplete, something that others would need whole books to develop. The moral function of art in White is to create absolutes – to intuit, imagine, or even more perversely, establish absolutes and then demolish them, re-establishing them *in absentia*. In a way, this is transcendental art par excellence, as in Paul Schrader's understanding of transcendental cinema: using the narrow possibilities of art to unveil the deep structures of experience.

White's writing constitutes a constant *mise en abyme*, a mirroring of its own mirroring, a play within a play, multiplied *ad infinitum*. It is the search for absolutes after the death of all gods which makes his novels sound like cries of broken statues, echoed in the lone and bare stretches of the sands of time. Ozymandias and Childe Harold together. Or, even closer to his heart, Werther and Faust.

White's novel search for the *isness* of manifold reality, as he struggles to explore and visualise its manifestations. The mysticism of the visible permeates his work, not simply because he loved William Blake (whose poetic language breathes throughout White's prose). The relationship between nouns and adjectives is probably the key to unlocking his alarming phrases: *green thought, yellow feelings, black gestures* – how can we read these two words together without being confused? *The blowfly on its bed of offal is but a variation of the rainbow*. This is extreme and provocative: you have to prepare yourself for entering, discreetly and with humility, somebody else's worlds, and struggle discreetly to find a place for yourself in there – but this is quite personal and, in a personal essay like this one, very few personal details matter.

I fell in love with his sentences after finishing *The Eye of the Storm*, for which I was told he received the Nobel Prize because his previous book, *The Vivisector*, was "too morbid." Shortly after, I read his European farewell elegy, *The Aunt's Story* (1948), which was quite different to his other books, a strange irregularity in which White competes anxiously with Dorothy M. Richardson, James Joyce, Gertrude Stein, Wyndham Lewis, Djuna Barnes and Virginia Woolf simultaneously, to write about psychological complexities, repressed desires and piquant details which he himself held in not very high regard.

As for his first books, *The Living and the Dead* (1941) and *Happy Valley* (1939), I read them much, much later – that's the best way. They exhibit a sardonic flippancy and witty intellectuality, the terrible levity with which the British bourgeoisie treats all serious questions under the simplistic rubric of common sense – something which, quite likely, White would have liked to forget in his later work. Indeed, *exhibit* is the word because, as the toils of a very young man, enmeshed still then in the narcissistic comforts of Anglocentric modernism, they are full of ostentatious truths grown in the gardens of the Bloomsbury circle, overblown high-classism pretending to be intellectual anxiety, and highly operatic moments that imitate the dramatic. *Too many styles in their sentences*, as White wrote later in a letter. Their perfected plots, with their puerile philosophical ruminations and their diluted James Joyce posturing, are somehow impressive and occasionally engaging, but needed to be reined by a unified vision which was not in the mind of the writer yet, or anymore, as the world around him was collapsing into the maelstrom of war.

Aldous Huxley said that the problem with novels is that they invent a cohesion that life itself does not possess. White's early novels are too novelistic, tidy, plot-driven – the original sin of all

Anglocentric writers. They lack *simplexity*: they want to complete and perfect what will always remain imperfect, irregular and unfinished. They imitate the real while being terrorised by reality. But as Robert Bresson pointed out in his *Notes on the Cinematograph*: "The true is inimitable, the false untransformable." You cannot imitate reality and you cannot transform its gaps. Only delusional puritans do not understand the paradox of greatness and wretchedness that simultaneously shape our realities. Indeed, the horrible truth is that the one feeds on the other, and the more real we become, the more able we are to do great good and perfidious evil.

You can only extrapolate from the real; if you try to make it better, you make it uglier, as it loses its solid form. It becomes a parody of itself, an imitation of an imitation, third from the truth, an illusion, a false prophecy, which is "the ultimate corruption of consciousness" – to use R.G. Collingwood's sublime expression. Or as Simone Weil said: I prefer a real hell from an imaginary paradise.

Why do we read White's early books? Because we want to see the world he was escaping from.

Entfremdungsgefühl and Torschlusspanik

The language of White's novels maps out a land of orality based on unpredicted, almost impromptu, voices and vocalisations. His uncomfortable sentences seem to expose the reader to the challenge of an existential elsewhere. Mnemonic imagination and photographic inventiveness alternate in White's sentences, framing a concrete language which gathers in itself various forms of dissonance and tension through the irregular flow of words. Its very concreteness makes it so hyper-real, so transparent and symbolic. Their very power as compact forms makes them appear de-realised, as if the representation of things that happen daily, from drinking milk to contemplating on an oiled newspaper or reading a volume from *The Decline and Fall of the Roman Empire*, lead to a new order of self-perception in a hyper-real state, like the one that led Sigmund Freud to his disturbance of memory on the Acropolis.

The feeling of derealisation, *entfremdungsgefühl*, is what White's works leave as an aftertaste in the mind of their readers. Miss Docker, Miss Quodling but also the character of all his characters, Sarsaparilla, "a fictitious outer suburb of Sydney," create the impression of an eerie and numinous reality hovering over them as an active presence within and between them. Things are so disturbing under the veneer of decency or the disguise of dark humour that, in the end, you simply can only distrust them. They disturb the reader's mind and create a sense of distance and self-distancing. As Freud would have said: *We really have come a long way!*

At the moment a book makes its readers momentarily forget that they are reading a book, suspending their reality principle and what they were taught to expect from reading, it points to an opening of vision beyond the strictures and satisfactions of habitual practices. White's ultimate legacy was given in 1987 when, like a sick Prospero, he put his magic wand down and simply farewelled writing, farewelled love, farewelled life: *Are you for magic? I am.* [...] *So I am for magic. For dream. For love. The pervasive dream which becomes more real than reality if we have faith in it. If we can resist abusing them, all our dreams can amount to a world faith. If we can pursue our dream of faith to the end, to the death if necessary.* His dialogue with Shakespeare becomes a dialogue with us: it presents our dreams not as escapism or evasion but as collective engagement, as our common destiny and bond. *Now I want / spirits to enforce, art to enchant / and my ending is despair, / unless I be relieved by prayer, / which pierces so that its assaults / mercy itself and frees all faults*, as the Bard announced it for all eternity.

This leads to the other dominant presence in his work, so elegantly expressed in his beloved German, with the peculiar term *torschlusspanik*. The whole of contemporary literature is *torschlusspanik*. White's novels are all about *torschlusspanik*. Kafka, Thomas Mann, Musil, Hemingway, Fitzgerald, Nadine Gordimer, Doris Lessing, J.M. Coetzee, Sebald, Cormac McCarthy are also about *torschlusspanik*.

The panic of the closed door, time is running out, you have no other chance, you are not going anywhere, no opportunity, no way out, no horizon. Nyctophobia, claustrophobia, egophobia, even phobophobia – all phobias together – are *torschlusspanik* in modern literature.

White is one of the first writers who sees that closed door, the absurdity of everyday experience, and yet desires to make some sense out of it. He is not toying with voguish panic or glamourising its mystique, as many contemporaneous existentialist writers and thinkers did world-wide then. Unlike Samuel Beckett, or his more recent American reincarnation Cormac McCarthy, White presents the absurd as the necessary background of all efforts for redemption and catharsis. He employs jokes, exorcisms, rituals, games, puns, the whole array of stratagems that the ancients used against the circularity of time, and the moderns use against the granularity of existence. And then he laughs at his own frivolity in expecting any form of closure.

After the dream

Whoever reads White's novels understands that the individual tone of his language makes you look around, because *everything lives outside the text.* No group, class or gender can usurp its specificity: *The Twyborn Affair* cannot give us a language for gender fluidity, nor *The Solid Mandala* a manifesto for gay liberation, nor *Voss* a narrative about Australian history, nor *The Tree of Man* a canon of Australian masculinity. White belonged to another generation, for whom sexuality was not a statement of ideological conformity or an act of social radicalism. In its clandestine privacy, it was sheer pleasure, cunning transgression and sometimes pure fun, instead of declaration of identity and performative obligation for political activism. His sexuality had nothing to do with contemporary ideas of identification. We identify with the person we are in love with, and not with an abstract idea of sexuality. The constant appeal to Michel Foucault and his unlovable and loveless sexualities, so easily adopted by the spectral identifications of postmodernity, cannot be seen anywhere in White's novels.

His homosexuality offered him an *ontological grounding* and a coded mythology, not stories for titillating adolescents and their hormonal rebellions under the false pretences of sexo-socialist revolutions. Foucault's half-baked ideas express the bane of the possessive individualism that has dominated Western European thinking since utilitarianism. White's most homosexual characters live in heterosexuality and vice versa: they move through genders, roles and behaviours exploring their limits and limitations. Indeed, their sexuality confuses them: they don't understand why they want to have sex, why they fail to fall in love, or why they fail to be loved. Human ambivalence toward our own body is probably the most radical aspect of these characters who do not exist in perpetual fake excitability, but experience their sexuality as just one aspect of their messy and confused existence: *The Twyborn Affair* is probably the most emblematic work on such interchangeability of gender.

His novels are all complex fairy tales that want to provoke by highlighting the afflictions they denote. The latent tradition they incorporate is not skin-deep: it raises possibilities beyond the realm of immediate existence – which explains why, again, archetypal criticism became so attached to them. His Aboriginal characters, like his European ones, belong to no specific historical age. They would be performing the same rituals fifteen or fifteen yeah I don't rough sorry no it won't Baker four hundred years ago, *mutatis mutandis*. They converse with Samuel Beckett *and* with the elders of their land. They come out of their dream-time, or the grand age of myths and fables, and go back there; they embody a certain disturbance in time and space and, after their mission is accomplished, they return to the abyss of fecund nothingness. But they leave traces behind, hand marks on the walls of time. White's characters feel the need to point out that probably there will always be something missing from the world – and that there is no way of finding it.

Redeeming the prototypes

In White's language, there is always an unexpected refraction, a twist in the symbolic connotations, which suspends all forms of identification. The "great Australian emptiness" is an emptiness of signifiers both within him and outside him. However, this is a problem beyond and above the act of writing. White never provided any key to the interpretation of his novels; the novels interpret themselves. *Sola scriptura* generates its interpretive frameworks and semantic references. Writers struggle with the inevitable inaccuracy of all natural languages. The idea that there will be a direct correspondence between words and things was abandoned even by Wittgenstein (probably even by the scholastics). The language of any individual adds a distinct, specific and personal inflection to the general irregularity of the connection between sentences and situations. No one else can adopt or adapt it; it brims with character and idiosyncrasy. It forcefully claims a space of semantic collision that can be harmonised only through the personality of the writer.

Sometimes, White's language is over the top (as they say locally), full of conscious exuberance; but that is only a façade. White made fun of the grand languages articulated by Proust or Tolstoy, Dostoevsky or Faulkner: he didn't want to have a totalising vision of existence, as all of them wished to construct. He was truly satisfied with the little crumps of infinity that his ordinary, quotidian characters present us with. His Augustinian, some would even call it Lutheran, anthropology is based on what is *missing* from the human phenomenon, not on what exists in abundance and excess. The Protestant in him sees life as intoxicating guilt and rapturous punishment; the writer sees all his characters as magnificent aberrations ready to be decapitated by a playful and nasty god, as is shown in Carl Dreyer's *Ordet* (1955) or Ingmar Bergman's *The Seventh Seal* (1957). The dark dance of imminent death is what gives his best novels a sense of drollness and cheerfulness. *In the midst of life we are in death*. This is not pessimistic or nihilistic: for

White this is engagement with the moment, our concern with time. At a certain stage, we must confront his Protestantism, so well hidden under his search for mystical experience, and so humanly underplayed by Veronica Brady in her great essays.

Protestantism is a truly wicked tradition, manifesting itself in all shades of black and deep blue, all degrees of depression and insanity. Its naïveté, expressed through its founding statement of *sola scriptura*, has bequeathed modernity and postmodernity the monumentally weird expectation of absolute and undisputed certainty. Its dark and sinister rationalism has nothing to do with the lucid and somehow jocular ideas of Aristotle, Thomas, Descartes or even the insane mental rigidity of Kant – philosophers who always left the back door of thinking open to imponderables and asymmetries. Wretched sinners in the hands of an angry God, Protestantism is probably the most narcissistic exhibitionism of self-aggrandisement that any religion has ever promulgated.

Recently, it has found its political translation into the domineering language of political correctness. One of its main tenets, somehow conveniently forgotten by contemporary activists, is the idea of *unconscious sin*, which has been reinvented today as the unconscious bias fad. White is aware of such fanciful delusions, so dominant in the era of social media: that other people can read your mind better than you can. His novels, especially after *The Tree of Man*, created an open-ended form of narrative unfolding that leaves everything in flux, and God in the perpetual limbo of humanity. He avoids the pernicious practice of the omniscient narrator. His narrative explores its themes while constructing its characters. It does not pretend to offer any closure or catharsis: for this reason, most of his "prose works" end abruptly in abeyance. They never offer a solution. The drama continues and *in the end there is no end.*

Against his own religious background, his novels are spaces of collisional anthropological structures, which sometimes can be read as metaphysical treatises on invisible deities. *Riders in the Chariot*, for example, poses a very important question: is there any sacredness left in a world of broken creatures? As James Joyce indicated, "history is a nightmare from which we try to awake" – but how? Maybe the most horrible nightmare is experienced in our illusion of being awake. White sensed every instance of this delusional character of experience, and never hesitated to point it out.

Such layering of his mythopoetic language created the ingeniously misleading interpretation of his works through Carl Jung's archetypes and the individuation process, starting with Andrew Riemer's initial reading in the late 1960s. Back then, it was groovy and chic to be Jungian, and for books be interpreted through archetypal criticism. Herman Hesse's magnificent fables suffered irreparably from such an approach.

This form of reading dominated the interpretation of his work for decades, until all Jungian reading became racist, homophobic, misogynistic (and many other horrible things) as judged by the puritans and the zealots of political correctness, or through the fanatical derangement of interpretive orthodoxies with their formulaic jargon. Certainly, there are serious problems with Jung's ideas, but they are not what these puritans denounce: all writing is made out of colliding signifiers and contested semantic fields. Ambiguity prevails and therefore only ambiguity matters.

White never intended to please or flatter the expectations of his readers, publishers or editors. He was one of the last writers whose sentences instilled fear into the mind; fear and awe, sometimes ecstasy. But mostly intimidation. Together with some central European writers, like Witold Gombrowicz and Hermann Broch, he is not afraid of berating his readers for their arrogance in believing that they can fully grasp the meaning of a work without themselves entering into the process of its construction – or, indeed, reconstruction. Today it is easy for critics and readers to deconstruct, because of the mechanical structure of writing. But at the moment you realise that a work of art is not only about its reception but its inception, then all critical certitudes and reader expectations collapse into absolute banalities.

After White, the benign figures of David Malouf, Thomas Keneally, Helen Garner, Sally Morgan or Kate Granville seem to walk alongside their readers, comforting their anguish and looking after their wounds. Malouf, for example, is the great classicist of contemporary literature. *An Imaginary Life* (1978) and *Ransom* (2009) show that his writing searches for the absolving myth of self-creation and self-invention beyond the restrictions of individualist understanding of the human self – so dominant in the English tradition. He anchored his writing to the great diachronic stories of self-articulation, with the lyricism and the transparency we find in John Williams, Robert Graves and Marguerite Yourcenar.

White belonged to the group of writers who made writing uncomfortable, delving into its harsh realities, as Barbara Baynton, Miles Franklin, Christina Stead or Henry Handel Richardson (amongst others) did. They exposed readers to psychological brutalities *within* their characters: their stories were not only about individuals rising up against social convention and oppression but, more importantly, against their own self-structure, against the internalised mask of their social reality which had become part of their existence and psyche. They exposed the fears, panics and insecurities in individuals, and made that the focus of the writing.

The lives of Stan Parker and Laura Trevelyan were not to be found out there, sublimated, sanitised or sensationalised; but within them, disparaging their excuses, fragmenting their personality and lacerating their body, as White would have said. This is the reason why his novels can never become tolerable Hollywood movies: they are raw and harsh and cannot create an atmosphere of communitarian cosiness. They remain texts without visual equivalence.

Fred Schepisi's adaptation of *The Eye of the Storm* (2011) shows how, with good intentions, you can transform White's stories into cartoons. The complexity of the characters who love their expensive mirror but hate the face they see in it cannot be adequately translated into the evil demon of images: language defends its polysemic structure, and images simply fail to frame the ambiguities and ambivalences of writing – that *odi et amo* in White's own psyche.

Because of these uncomfortable realities, the narrative turns itself outward and searches, for its references, to the landscapes in which stories take place. Like the prophets of the Hebrew Bible who always hear but never see God, White records vocal vibrations with the hyper-sensitivity of a loner who wants to start a conversation with everything around him: the weather, the city, the buildings, the clothes, the garbage bins, the animals, the flowers, the colours, the shoes, the cars – all the natural and social phenomena. Characters disrupt this conversation and need to be bypassed or silenced. All his novels end with images or intimations of a cosmic redemption which does not encompass humans. Most of the novels end with the epic struggle of objects to survive their abuse by humans. All human beings, on the other hand, are punished to remain in transit into the eternal limbo of doubt created by their consciousness and crystallised by their individuality.

The spectre of Jean-Jacques Rousseau's unreflexive primitivism seems to haunt the emotional structures of White's characters, undermining their flimsy self-justifications. Nature versus Culture seems to consume them with dilemmas of self-purification and cleansing. But these outcomes never eventuate: in a world of filth, you can never be clean. But filth is good; it fertilises and disgusts at the same time. White the moralist could not find another way: full of contradictions and self-negations, struggling for a sense of unity and purpose which he knew he could never have. Filth is good, though: fertile and ugly, fecund and abhorred. This is how you create subversive signifiers in a culture that sees itself predominantly in utilitarian terms and demands from everyone, even from a novelist, that they meet expectations. It is good only because it is *not* useful.

White announces that your anxieties and failures are more important than any recognition or success. Only the vanquished make history: the victors write rhetorical, self-congratulatory chronicles. Because of this, which he evokes in so many of the quotes at the beginning of his books, you know: there will be no atonement, no closure, no redemption. Blasphemy begins with the truth: who can confront the realisation that truth leads to sadness and melancholia, not freedom or fulfilment?

Truth never sets you free: it binds you within your limitations, it shows you what you are not. And who wants to renounce the infantilising omnipotence that modern societies instil in the mind or psyche of us all? Many have tried to eliminate such unsettling ideas from the interpretation of his work. And they de-historicised its references, de-temporalized its symbolism, destructured its architecture. Of course, we will ask: what is truth? That's the old question we have already found in this discussion: but if Jesus was unable to answer for the hungry mind of the eternal sceptic in us, who back then was called Pontius Pilate, how could we? I hate repeating myself; yet this has nothing to do with me. Or maybe it has?

The Attack of the Insipids

The age of archetypal interpretations passed when the postmoderns conquered Western intellectual discourses. What in the 1960s was considered liberating and revolutionary became colonialist, patriarchal and Eurocentric. Certain critics in the 90s – and we will find them still mentally living in that decade – like Simon During and *tanti quanti* have created a cultural demonology, a *Malleus Maleficarum* of ultra-sophisticated, meaningless criticism which prosecutes the bewitchment of literature by denouncing its meta-ethical claims and valuations.

All is publicity and posturing for During: the commercialisation of a mystique which is nothing more than pretentious camp, a gay cabal for Kabbalistic homosexuals. Nothing more than fanciful stories for the bourgeois dilletantes who like clandestine sexual perversions and narcissistic self-promotion. During wrote a perfectly deranged study of White's novels. Juxtapose it with Mark Williams' balanced critical exploration, and you have the perfect monument to the world of hysterias and obsessions imposed by scholars who have lost the ability to understand what Milan Kundera called the "art of the novel."

During's approach managed, for some time, to strip literary writing of all its intricacies, and abolish the space in which reading could open up emancipatory questions about meaning. Is there a class for this text? Are snobbish homosexuals the only 'community' who read White's novels? In the end, there was an end: readers lost the ability to express their personal responses to the uncomfortable conversations of certain texts, and all interpretive activity was imprisoned within the professional communities of vocational narcissists.

Academia was taken over by intellectual *bon-viveurs* and of Francomaniac flaneurs. White's novels "do not help to produce good citizens or a good society," as the microphysics of institutional power would have wanted. That's Foucault, always lurking behind a meaningless rhetoric with his grandiloquent platitudes. Good citizens and good society: Foucault must have stolen this, as so many other ideas, from Dante's Paradiso.

Certainly, such mundane scholasticism is not enough to explore or, indeed, validate the idiosyncrasy of White's work, or account for its specificity. In reality, individuation has taken place at an even deeper level than Jungian theorists could imagine. It was a process of reassembling language to mirror a grammar of existence that was emerging and was still uncrystallised at the time of its writing. The continuous struggle of White to bring experience under the protective shield of language is a parameter that never left his personal style: the incommunicability and ineffability of experience was to be transformed into a linguistic map, a verbal mandala, to elucidate the actuality of existence.

In itself, existence is ambiguous, polysemic and, most importantly, traumatised and fragmented; no sense can be made of the trauma of being yourself in a world of alienation, as the Marxists called it, or in an acosmic pluriverse of contradictions, as the metaphysicians claimed. In a slim volume from

1980, Brian Kiernan adequately framed these unresolved issues between the reader and White's books – and his study must be read again today.

White's semantic spaces were constantly mutating, while struggling for the solidity of a classical form. His writing, in its continuity, struggled but not always succeeded in creating a formal equivalent for the inability of human to know themselves. Sometimes this process becomes truly annoying and exasperating; condemning a society, as a puritan moralist, for its erratic unconscious, while forgetting that unconscious is, in itself, erratic, timeless and evasive. But White returned to Australia with the traumatised mind of someone who had lost faith in his own humanity. The experience in the Middle East during World War II was a time of existential rupture – and it took him almost ten years to regain his ability to confront the solidity of the real and discover its moral ambiguities.

His is the lonely voice of the 'prodigal son' who went through the maelstrom of European wars and came to confront his own temptation: "the Great

Australian emptiness." Emptiness but not ordinariness, as During misread it. What, in the beginning, started as existential numbness morphed into a romantic vision of a man against a whole continent, who writes stories about the land not by reading Marcus Clarke or Rolf Boldrewood, but after listening to Mahler and Liszt or by looking at Delacroix's and William Blake's paintings. It was also the vision of a continent instilling you with the dark premonition that it is not yours: a continent that you took violently from someone who was weaker than you. Therein lies the moral dilemma for the writer. How can the crime be perceived? Or: how can the criminal atone?

The trauma of being-elsewhere became an opening for the here-now. This made it possible to allow the invisible presences of the Aborigine, the migrant, the illegal alien to emerge as literary themes in their complex and confused interiority as human beings, not as political statements and caricatures. The pervasive, diffused idea that there is something negative in them, both as creative rebellion and self-consuming fear, makes his books a space of intense ambivalence.

Stan Parker is the great embodiment of the other, the outcast, the stranger in the land he inhabits. And yet he struggles to populate it with his sweat and tears, in short, with his life. But there are so many invisible presences around him, that he feels their existence without the words to vocalise them. Voss is another embodiment, together with his companions: Le Mesurier, for instance, and his illuminations in the desert. The indeterminate hunch and longing that spur humans on – while simultaneously blinding them and throwing them into the prison of their own will – are constantly framed by White, but never clearly articulated and therefore essentialised. They are *omens* in search of their *numinosity*. People are drawn to their names. Laura Trevelyan, who are you? Theodora Goodman can you please explain yourself? Ellen Roxburgh, what does the song for your delivery actually mean?

The characters are all compelled to become their names. Ultimately, each name is not an identifier but a destiny. In the end, the anonymous flesh emerges from the words and builds its dominion amongst us. We are all bothered by the presence of such people. They become, in our minds, our legends.

Something personal, again

Hi hi nine I really need it later no I'm Robia see arm modem born promise become okay creator okay going for a walk or not okay Bendigo that was good to come. At this point, I must disrupt my lofty ruminations. Several years after my silent landing on the continent, I translated two of his novels, one play and some essays into Greek. I vividly remember Paul Brennan giving me, as a present, the volume he edited, *Patrick White Speaks* (1992), with the admonition to look carefully into the mind of this (as he stressed) brilliant and cranky man. So, many decades later, I still feel the excitement and the sense of accomplishment that I experienced when I finished translating *Voss* in 1993, a book that I keep reading again and again. How did I manage that? I ask myself to this day.

On the miniature screen of a prehistoric Mac, I squinted my eyes so persistently that I developed a detached retina and, more painfully, as I folded my feet, I suffered a fractured knee cap: not a small price to pay, especially when you aren't doing it for money, and you work purely for the pleasures and challenges of translation.

Later, when the Australia Council for the Arts introduced a translation grant scheme, I applied for the translation of *A Cheery Soul*, which Max Mastrosavas from Adelaide wanted to perform in Greek. How I managed to translate the impeccable phrase, *I never knew before … but 'dog' is a 'god' turned around*, or *In the world of light, I am darkness. The ghosts of ideas struggle to escape out of this obscure mind*, or many others like it, puzzles me to this day. Translation leads to an intimate and deeply personal engagement with the text. You even find yourself crying as you struggle with language which begs to migrate from one printed page to another.

Later, after I finished, things became even more complicated. Then I had to think of the practicalities: the publisher, the editor and the audience, even the reviewers. The initial magic was gone, and the sublime moments of rupture and anticipation vanished under the expectations for a successful, sellable book. *Voss* did okay. There was a story there, developing in a linear fashion, and it had lots of drama.

When I began translating *The Vivisector*, everything was confusing. Nothing worked in Greek. The sentences sounded clumsy. The images, grotesque. The music of words had no melodic threads. I had to re-write parts of the novel, through a process of acculturating it to the novelistic expectations of Greek readers. In the end, I projected onto the text my own anxieties about writing, about reading, about thinking, and so many other things. The prospective publisher asked me: Have you forgotten your Greek? Three or four years wasted. So much effort and sweat. I was walking up and down Glebe Point Road in Sydney testing out the music of the translated texts, invoking the airy nothing to inhabit my sentences. But I felt deserted and graceless.

In any case, the translation is lost somewhere. The first publisher found the novel morbid and unreadable. The other, who liked and wanted to publish it, died unexpectedly, and the files were destroyed when his basement was flooded by rain. I think that I must translate it again, after so many years of re-reading it in different circumstances. But it was the roaring Keating era, the time of the Redfern speech, and of triumphant multiculturalism, which kept me in the continent – oh, those were the days, the unfulfilled 90s, the last renaissance before the great endarkenment. The era of high hopes, illusions of omnipotence and euphoric Utopianism. The era preparing for the rise of insignificance and the domination of velvet totalitarianism.

During the period, at a Greek-Australian studies conference in Melbourne in 1994, I gave a paper on White's work and its translation problems. Some attendants laughed loudly every time I mentioned the name of Manoly Lascaris. A young, then upcoming writer poked fun at me. *Who reads such books?* He was loudly talking to some other presumably left-wing writers who made a profitable career full of awards, by exoticizing ethnics and presenting caricatures as authentic representations of marginality. They were giggling and chuckling and, halfway through the lecture, made their grand exit from the university hall, making sure they were noticed by everyone. Was this the defiance of rebellious youth, or the narcissism of privileged ignorance? I never understood which it was, until I later read some of their stuff.

But I was not discouraged. And I said to myself that White's work must be read in its entirety, and as a whole. That's the only way to appreciate the continuous unfolding of its investigation into the existential openings of language, the potentialities of narrative mythopoetics and *the struggle to create new forms out of the rocks and sticks of words.* The problem, I guess, with many specialised readers was mostly with the verb 'to create', as modern cultural studies prescribed the death of the author and its replacement by the legendary dominance of writing or whatever other structure writes the writing of its writing. Such convenient structuralism was propagated by Barthes who, even when he visited Japan, couldn't see a country, a culture or individuals, but a system of signs. French provincialism at its peak: I cannot find my Parisian croissant in Tokyo, because everything there is dematerialised.

Even Mr Lascaris can be seen as a system of signs from this perspective. But what kind of sign system is a human being? *What* was Mr Lascaris? The conundrums of thinking, which are also paradoxes and contradictions, transform the irreducible singularity of an individual into a system of representation, a field of flowing references without a centre, as eloquent post-modernists declare. But was Mr. Lascaris a field and a rhizome? Or a destination and a destiny? An accidental meeting that led to a life-long destiny? We must come back to him.

White's dilemma took new directions when he decided to create new forms. You need imagination to discover reality; otherwise, the real remains amorphous and formless, a jelly fish and an octopus, escaping capture by slipping away. Only through imagination can we find a local habitation and a name for what is everyday ours, and yet remains constantly beyond us. White tamed music through visual means; not only because he was a painter *manqué*, as they called him. This is the destiny of prose: to verbalise rhythms. The early Hemingway knew this; so did Gertrude Stein and James Joyce. This element makes *Voss* so distinct: *When they opened us with knives, they took out our hearts. Some wore them in their hats, some pressed them to keep for ever, some were eating them as if they have been roses, all with joy, until it was realised the flesh had begun to putrefy. Then they were afraid. They hung their flowers upon a dark tree, quickly, quickly.*

This passage must be *heard* again and again: it's a violin sonata.

But why?

It is obvious that White *wants* to alienate his readers. He doesn't want an empathic identification with his characters; the story is more important than them. "Never trust the teller, trust the tale," as D.H. Lawrence advised. The characters move the story forward, but they are not the full story: their unconscious conversations, unseen settings, and implied subtexts, are the story. Each of his novels, especially of the 1960s and 70s, is constructed around an extended but invisible set of plots and subplots, all forming together a prismatic, multi-layered narrative, mostly without closure or catharsis. The *abeyant end* is one of the most impressive elements in White's novels. Yes, the end of *The Tree of Man* offers probably the wisest lines ever written by a novelist: *So that in the end there were the trees. The boy walking through them with his head drooping as he increased in stature. Putting out shoots of green thought. So that, in the end, there was no end.*

White didn't want to exoticize, to create picturesque postcards, either of happy idylls or of Gothic misery, for the Australian experience. His Australian cosmos is entropic: it is turned against itself – and it celebrates self-destructive tendencies.

Most writers who visited and wrote about Australia dealt with its realities as the backdrop for their personal ennui or thrill-seeking adventurism. You have this feeling with Lawrence, for example, or Chatwin and Bill Bryson when they write about Australia. Even with classical writers like Mark Twain and Anthony Trollope. (Only Charles Darwin's memories of the country are narratives of cruel dissection, in a strangely fascinating style.)

Many travellers visited the place for two months and thought that they extracted its perennial truths through their encounters with taxi drivers, hotel owners or some random meetings at the bus stop or the local pub – places where people usually put on masks and pretend to be somebody else or want to escape their everyday reality and make up stories. Through hasty and blurry snapshots, many writers on holidays want to construct an outlandish Utopia. Their Australia is a fantasy of cultural, sexual or anti-social escapism in which everything is bigger and better or smaller and pettier than the same things in the village they came from.

The background of the uncanny Aboriginal presence also gives the strange certainty that travellers participate in an exciting cosmic drama which could sell well when promoted by an entrepreneurial publisher, offering the necessary escapism from middle-class boredom through the exoticism of multicultural folklore. This can be seen in cinema, for example, in Nicolas Roeg's *Walkabout* (1971) and Ted Kotcheff's *Wake in Fright* (1971), both made by visiting adventurists. In them, the Australian irregularity becomes truly gory and frightening, but not in the ways that Lawrence's bush is menacing and sinister. As tourists, these filmmakers want to be terrorised by Australia. *Wolf Creek* (2005), *Razorback* (1984), *The Reef* (2010), *Roadgames* (1981) and many more are about the wonderful tortures and exquisite death that the continent provides its naïve, unsuspected and repressed visitors. Even *Mad Max*, parts one (1979) and second (1982), promises fear and suffering – and even more than that, sexualised with leather clothes and phallic motorcycles.

In that context, we can situate *Riders in the Chariot* and *The Twyborn Affair*. How can we account for such cutting-edge cultural and historical reflexivity in a continent so majestically *sauvage* and wonderfully naïve? Holocaust survivors in God's paradise? Transgendered identities in the land of perennial essences? White's vision gently removes expectations about cultural and intellectual realities. It's his vision of a world *within* this world that redeems social anxiety through the unconditional affirmation of the human condition. In his world, all endure the same destiny: blacks, whites, migrants, women, homosexuals, and everything they cherish, are all perfected through their weakness. Their world is broken, their body is crumbling, their mind is imploding, but they abide: "Perplexed but not driven to despair; persecuted, but not forsaken; struck down, but not destroyed" according to the old apostle.

Such transgressive mortality asks and yearns for a transgressive manifestation. And transgressive means flawed. But if you read a book and constantly search for awkward moments, it's like making love and trying to find imperfections on your lover's body. From the first paragraph in each of his works, it's obvious that White's writing is not the usual style we find in British, or even in American and Canadian, writers.

White was inspired by the promethean ambition to re-invent English or, at least, to write *singular* English in order to emancipate local literature from the grand dynasty of Great British tradition and its canonical writers as defined by the educational criteria of F.R. Leavis. His writing exuded the peculiar sense of moving between all of this, between experimentation and tradition, between novelty and order, structure and formlessness. It was a writing of dilemmas and abeyances, not of answers and statements.

Initially, my shallow Mediterranean scepticism was confronted by the strong, stark, robust idiolect of his sentences. Beyond the storyline, there was something disturbing and disorderly in the tone of his narratives and the rhythm of his phrases, something extremely artificial and unnatural – so much so, it made feel me bad as a reader, that I was obviously missing something. On such occasions, all of us from the Middle Sea rush back to our great, unsurpassed, soothing fairy tales of yore: *The Iliad* for example, which I read every time I lose faith and courage, or *The Odyssey*, which I revisit whenever the news is depressing and demoralising. Yet, after reading White, I returned to the most sublime Mediterranean classic, Dante's *The Divine Comedy*. Dante re-assured me that there is an implicit order behind the chaotic iconographies of imagination, something in which I, the reader, was necessary and somehow inevitable, although I couldn't see it. But I had to follow the path of self-discovery through the exploration of other selves and other individuals.

In contrast, White's prose re-arranges reading habits; it provokes, it unsettles, it confuses. And all of this in a very subtle, indirect and imperceptible manner. It makes you feel unwelcome, keeps you out of the story. Some readers like being confused. I have never liked smooth, elegant, chiselled prose: I read Graham Greene, Evelyn Waugh, Nadine

Gordimer, John Fowles, Patrick Modiano, Claude Simon, J.M. Coetzee, John Updike, Philip Roth amongst many others – and I read them carefully and systematically, struggling to find a redeeming sentence, a phrase which will make their reading the ultimate gift of grace, but to no avail. Cormac McCarthy also comes to mind here: his troubled, elliptical, frustrating prose, with novelistic structures in search of their centre, as in *Blood Meridian* (1985) – a quality that can be also felt in only a few other works, such as Marilynne Robinson's *Gilead* (2004) and V.S. Naipaul's *A House for Mr Biswas* (1961). But no. Only Yourcenar's *Memoirs of Hadrian* (1951) offers me the great gift of attunement to my own sense of time.

These are writers who do not project onto their story the flaws of their existence: they struggle with them, sometimes denounce them, and show the struggle with their own mind to the reader. At other times, they are fascinated by these flaws and use them as a lens to recalibrate the horizon of their own mythopoetic structures; they are mostly interested in the story and not in themselves, the storyteller. They do not want to expose themselves or represent a community they belong to, according to the political and the commercial labelling of the day. ("I may be homosexual, but I am not gay," as White once said – and definitely he was not queer.) In the absence of grand narratives of collective recognition, auto-fictionalisation, the dominant form of writing today, has become a completely different genre. It is not autobiography but self-dramatization.

For example, White's *Flaws in the Glass* is a confusing autobiographical narrative because of its self-sufficiency: it does not pretend to be anything else but a 'self-portrait.' It doesn't even claim to shed light on or interpret his novels. It simply talks about Patrick White and his significant other: it is a narrative about the artist as a human being, not as writer, philosopher, activist, lover or partner. It is unlike Sartre's *The Words* or Karen Blixen's *Out of Africa* (1937), Nabokov's *Speak, Memory* or Gertrude Stein's *The Autobiography of Alice B. Toklas* (1933) or, indeed, a book that I profoundly admire, Kazantzakis' *Report to Greco*.

Despite the multi-awarded, self-aggrandising mania of today, which abolishes empathic imagination, the most difficult narrative venture is to talk about the great unknown of your existence, your own self. Because the writer must have a self in order to lose it through imagining, and then try to retrieve it through writing. In his book, White struggles to regain his commonness, his triviality, his mundaneness. He knows that his novels, their interpreters and the Nobel prize have elevated him to the status of a cultural icon.

He wants to debunk the perception that he is exceptional, or is in a metaphysical engagement with writing, excavating the truth or memory for us, the *hoi polloi*. Through trivialities and banal episodes, full of sarcasm and self-irony, he rebuilds the living space which belongs absolutely and totally to him. Even if he publishes it, he wants other people to feel empowered to talk about their unremarkable and prosaic ordinariness. His prophets write their cosmic pronouncements on dunny walls, because their very name is their own wound: Hurt-le. Or, indeed, Man-oly.

The unsentimental reconstruction of moments of bliss and discomfort, or episodes of illumination and wretchedness – all at the same time – makes *Flaws in the Glass* so pregnant with narrative openings. *The puritan in me has always wrestled with the sensualist. As a child I felt ashamed of my parent's affluence. I was aware of a formless misery as well as material distress the other side of the palisade protecting the lives of the favoured few. For that reason, I have never been able to enjoy what any 'normal' member of my parent's class considers his right. What is seen as success, my own included, has often filled me with disgust.* Such existential ambivalence towards his own self, the *odi et amo* moments addressed to his very reality, make White's prose so challenging and bewildering. When we usually read autobiographies, we want to find an interpretive background, a cadre of references that localise and locate the words and ideas put forward.

Unlike Nabokov, for example, and his immense ego-love, White presents what is wrong with himself, the real and mainly imaginary flaws that defined his material and symbolic life. You cannot construct a hermeneutical framework on such shaky and self-defeating foundations. It is also interesting that his imaginary flaws are more interesting and serious than the actual ones: the Dostoevskyan impulse to feel as a transcendental criminal against whom the whole universe has conspired lies at the heart of every artist. But what is his cosmic crime? Is it his sexuality, his erotics? High-class consciousness and male privilege? Or, maybe, his inability to believe and trust, or have faith? As Buddha said: "If I don't descend into Hell, who will?"

It is quite difficult to follow his meandering thoughts, which do not try to glorify the complexities of his mind, celebrate his sexuality or fetishize the conflicts of his psyche, but simply to expose the pedestrian, tedious character of his chaotic existence. Yet these thoughts are surrounded by mystery; and when White isn't ready, or is looking elsewhere, then they strike hard: *Till he began to know every corner of the darkness, as if it were daylight, and he were in love with the heaving world, down to the last blade of wet grass.* And soon

– which can be years later, because you have to be old, sick and receptive – the real message is given, the final step on the ladder of transformation: *Then the old man, who had been cornered long enough, saw, through perversity perhaps, but with his own eyes. He was illuminated. He pointed with his stick at the gob of spittle. "That is God," he said.*

Even if you do not search for God, God will find you. You expect the emissary to be a Hamlet, a Nikolai Stavrogin or an Adrian Leverkühn, but the good news, in the end, is given by a vagabond, a bus conductor or a hairdresser. Nothing exceptional or charismatic, significant or deviant, horrible or sublime. Everything is suspended in time and place: all characters live in expectation. Something is going to happen which will change everything; but nothing happens and all characters return to their creative confusion, captives of repetition and routine, while occasionally exploding into moments of painful and demoralising illumination: *Words were not the servant of life, but life, rather, was the slave of words.* Nothing more disheartening and demoralising than that.

From the beginning, White had no illusions, Utopian ideals or great revolutionary plans; he didn't also have the scepticism of old age, not even of mature age. Why? Some would claim that it was his sexuality, the unnameable vice that killed Oscar Wilde – a terrifying presence still dominant in the colony of the 1950s and 60s. In reality, his sexuality was both a source of inspiration and self-restriction, as he experienced through it the most extreme and expansive emotions that any human would want to have: the need for self-degradation through vulgarity and grossness, and the longing for redemption and grace through devotion and attachment. And, of course, all the in-between lapses and relapses, decisions and reversals, ups and downs. Mr Lascaris, again.

The unidentifiable

Most English writers play it safe: based on the hegemonic position of English, they want immediate success, instant recognition – and awards. In order to achieve this, they remain obedient to the great seductress of writing: grammar. Their books are re-written by their publishers, editors and public relations personnel. At the end of the production line, they are not the books that the writers had in mind or wanted to write. They are products of the publishing industry, and most of them are written with the desire to become movies. They are scripts for Hollywood, for a committee of screenwriters who will transform the language of the novel into a visual simulacrum of its meaning.

That's not the case with White. I read somewhere that, after sending the manuscript to his publishers, he never allowed a single comma to be changed. It is so refreshing and enabling: his voice is unmediated and undomesticated –unedited is the right word. It is *his* voice which comes through to the reader loud and clear, with all its annoying inflections and refractions. It echoes his own struggle with language and his desire to invent a form of writing as the converging space of the imaginary and the recollected, but in a language as distinctly spoken in the colony. Most crucially, it indicates a struggle to construct a narrative voice, a narrator, an authorial presence, which will invisibly animate the dramaturgy and make the story a space of foreboding and imminence – but in the way that Catholic theologians perceive *immanent grace*. The author is nowhere until he is actualised by the reader – especially the synergistic readers, who search for encounters.

There is *someone* in his sentences who remains undefinable and unnameable. Despite their concreteness, his sentences also frame a diffuse and indistinguishable *nothing* which pulsates to be born. Shakespeare wrote his famous lines: *The poet's eye, in fine frenzy rolling, / doth glance from heave to earth, from earth to heaven; / And as imagination bodies forth / the forms of things unknown, the poet's / turns them to shapes and gives to airy nothing / a local habitation and a name.* The Bard was actually talking about writing as a process of imaginative naming and abiding, indeed homing.

In White's novels, there are always certain imperceptible dynamics that the writer keeps at the threshold of understandability. He doesn't want to name the *nothingness* that permeates the structures of emotions and patterns of storytelling. This diffuse emptiness denotes the hidden elements of numinosity and unworldliness that emerge, now and then, in his stories. How can you write realistic novels without realistic features? By hyper-realising the story and its action, White transforms the realistic background into a magical fairy tale: he uses the morphology of fairy tales to denote what is missing from the stories, the absences that are felt but never mentioned. This also accounts for the strong references to mysticism that we find, especially at the beginning of most of his novels, which must be used as signposts toward the core of the story.

Very few writers have ever achieved this. Probably Proust is the most obvious. In his long-winded sentences, the reader expects to find an unconcealed reality or secret, only to realise that the secret was too obvious all along: the sentences themselves. *Longtemps, je me suis couché de bonne heure. Parfois, à peine ma bougie éteinte, mes yeux se fermaient si vite que je n'avais pas le temps de me dire: "Je m'endors."* The sentence is strong enough to carry the weight of the many volumes that followed. From previous writers, another point of reference is Gustave Flaubert. In his best books, the sentence that begins the story is the musical scale around which theme and variations are constantly enacted. *Comme il faisait une chaleur de 33 degrés, le boulevard Bourdon se trouvait absolument desert*, he writes in the very first line of *Bouvard et Pécuchet*. And carries on: *Deux hommes parurent. L'un venait de la Bastille, l'autre du Jardin des Plantes.* We need to know nothing else: everything else follows the pattern of intonations and evocations that we find in these foundational sentences, full of pragmatic details and sensory connotations.

White emancipated Australian English without transforming it to an oddity or an exotic cliché. Writers like Christina Stead, Clive James, Peter Carey, Tim Winton and Richard Flanagan have domesticated their prose for an audience addicted to the demonstrative one-dimensionality of immersive journalism, formed by the language of contemporary media. They followed the Americans like Tom Wolfe, Truman Capote, Joan

Didion, or even Norman Mailer and Michael Herr, who dispensed of all imaginative landscapes for the sake of subjectivised emotionalism and the cult of *docufiction*. White speaks constantly about the burial of feeling under the garlands of journalistic prose and denounces the strictures of pseudo-realism that dominated writing in the 1950s and 60s. In his last books, he made some concessions to such realistic conventions, until he totally disparaged these concessions in *Memoirs of Many in One* – a book which is substantially unreadable, because of the way it dismantled the conventions of writing novels.

However, when we read *The Vivisector* we become able to follow the intricacies of the development, the lines of writing White pursued and continued, as well as those he abandoned. The novel is dense, off-putting, somehow turgid, but self-contained, semantically complex and psychologically confusing: it sets its own limits and remains within them. It makes no other claims than those made by writers who want to explore new and "original" semantic thresholds. We know that there are models for Hurtle Duffield: *peintres maudits*, some of them intimately known by White. Francis Bacon, for example, hovers around like a malevolent angel: his panel *Three Studies for Figures at the Base of a Crucifixion* (1944) blesses the entire repertoire of imagery with its blasphemous and miasmatic dis-beautification. There is something rotten in the kingdom of images, and the painter foregrounds this visual stench and disfigurement. One of the preceding mottos comes for the great: *the great Invalid, the great Criminal, the great Accursed One – and the Supreme Knower. For he [reached] the Unknown* – the *puer aeternus*, Arthur Rimbaud.

The Vivisector is the ultimate example of this exploration of the Unknown, essentially of the unknowable explorer. More than the exuberant prophecies of *Riders in the Chariot* or the hermaphroditic fantasies of *The Twyborn Affair*, there is something peculiarly anti-prophetic, almost barbaric in its pages. It explores what happens to an individual when he loses all sense of being welcome in the world, and the world becomes a negative place to be in. It is a simple case of alienation (as

Karl Marx claimed), or de-worldification (as Martin Heidegger proclaimed). How do we experience the self as an *a-cosmic anomie*? The acosmic is also uniconic: chaos cannot be iconised. It remains in a state of formless potentiality: everything is possible but nothing is concrete, therefore visible and shareable.

Art is a tragic defence mechanism which shields Hurtle Duffield from the nothingness of being thrown into existential anomie. He is forced to become like God, especially to become a God unto himself. Salvation, or even better redemption, come through colours and their combinations, their unforeseen nuances – because colours have a life of their own and hence vivify the bodies that will be dissected alive by God, or by readers. White uses art to confront the enigma of existential randomness, the Heideggerian *Geworfenheit* in the beloved absurdity of the shared world. In a way, he is close to André Malraux's idea of art as anti-destiny: a conscious way out of natural determinism and an opening up to the idea of purposeful living.

White actually discovers that, under everything beautiful or reassuring, there lurks something terrible and horrifying: a miasma, or even an evil presence that cannot be understood or tamed. Duffield realises that the struggle to depict beauty brings out the criminal in him (and in us), creating an opening for everything anti-beautiful to emerge. So, *The Vivisector* is about human anxiety in a world without imminent or expected redemption. It confronts head on Marcel Proust's world, which is also John Ruskin's world and the world of Oscar Wilde as well as the world of so many French prose writers – the world of frustrated lovers with their painful evasions. But the trajectory of White's book is convoluted: you must first be an aesthete and have been wholeheartedly seduced by the refinement and the elegance of artifice, in order to denounce aestheticism. The ultimate form of aestheticism is to compile an encomium to ugliness: first, of course, you have to experience ugliness, and this is not pleasant, and not easy even to talk about.

I read *The Vivisector* many times after I translated it. Twenty-five years ago, it rekindled in me the flames of an aestheticist vision of experience. I didn't realise that aestheticism had influenced my mind so deeply after my youthful forays into Walter Pater, Ruskin, Baudelaire, Mallarmé, Wilde and the early Yeats. I thought they had been obliterated from my memory. Well, there was Proust, always Proust, who made me feel the frisson of sublime art, together I admit, *mea culpa*, with the Russian symbolists, Andrey Belly and Vassily Rozanov. And how could anyone escape Thomas Mann's vision of lethal beauty in *Death in Venice* (1912)? Only the colour-blind and the Calvinists could manage that. We are all Platonists at heart, pretending to subscribe to the trivialities of the dominant, insane, British empiricism, or the self-obvious, irrational truths of American pragmatism – while thinking of *the Divine Destroyer* and searching for the strange *creature, not quite man, not quite god, who will heal the wounds.*

Frequently, as for years I tried to sleep after midnight, I reflected on Proust's observation that *a picture's beauty does not depend on the things portrayed in it*. It had impregnated me with the horror of a beauty totally imperceptible, not simply because *beauty is the beginning of the terrible*, but because it is elusive, transformable, and does not abide permanently in anything. The Greeks knew this, as well as the Romans, and the Renaissance Italians, and also the Chinese and Japanese. Murasaki Shikibu wrote the most sustained treatise on the ways that fiction can nail down beauty's fleeting emergence. These are inceptions which appear, disappear and re-appear centuries later, under different skies, in order to be forgotten again; and they remain hidden in the pages of a book until someone unexpectedly finds a copy in a provincial bookshop, and resurrects them.

Despite the romanticised mythology, no genius ever had a glimpse, let alone a full experience, of beauty. Geniuses hallucinate and willingly fall prey to their own illusions – in exactly the same way that the postmodernists who deny beauty fall prey to their own follies. But beauty is a destructive force beyond the aesthetics of the objects or words that embody it, beyond even the minds that are aware of it. Beauty is liminal: it presupposes a huge catastrophe, and an imploding psyche. In the opening created by such implosion, the primordial *das es* emerges: the pre-rational, unverbalised and uniconic being of the self. It is a rhythm, a personal tone, the surplus semantics of the incommunicable I: the elements detected in any work of human hands that cannot be reduced to, or deduced from, the particulars of its context.

And beauty doesn't last long: it turns against itself. Through the art object, only the incomplete and *chaosmic* nature of the human being comes out, not any implied harmony and order. Life is under-determined, not over-determined as French Marxists once so erroneously and narcissistically claimed. Random, unpredicted factors appear to interrupt the plausibility of all convenient assumptions. The great ideal of all Western thinking, the self, is only a brief moment of repose. More specifically, it is the product of being perpetually in a vertigo, unable to understand what just happened or to predict what happens next, caught *in the dizzy course of perpetual becoming*, as White announces at the end of one his short stories.

The becoming, again; we inhabit a formless void through which the foundational cry of all beginnings has not yet been uttered: *be light made*. But the self in perpetual becoming is also a self in never-ending angst: it faulters, collapses and re-emerges because of its tendency to split itself, to falsify its very memory, ultimately remaining silent when confronted by the question of its own truth. The most interesting of White's characters are the evil ones, always tempted by goodness. How can we see and understand goodness as temptation? Can we ever visualise the illusive form of goodness beyond the sugary Renaissance angels or kitschy Hollywood caricatures? Or, indeed, evil beyond the horned demons of folk mythologies or the Nietzschean will for annihilation?

Maybe the original struggle for survival left behind the traces of the murderer, the cannibal and the predator; while in that mess, the mind thinks, imagines and cries only for love, humility, compassion. Thucydides, Machiavelli, Hobbes and Freud were puzzled and annoyed by the involuntary tendency of people to do good deeds and dream of reconciliation, equilibrium, *gelassenheit* – Eliot's moment in the rose garden. Tempted by goodness and unsurprised by joy: herein lies the key to White's mythopoetics. He called it *the signs of life* and gave them a name, Mrs Godbold, in *Riders in the Chariot*: *Mrs Godbold could not help admiring the houses for their signs of life: for the children coming home from school, for a row of young cauliflowers, for a convalescent woman, who had stepped outside in her dressing gown to gather a late rose.* This is ecstatic realism, sublime, ineffable. The beyond within the banal.

However, the tragic dramatist in him tries to cope with the consequences of the certainty that we will never know ourselves, and that we will never achieve the goodness that makes us be who we are. What is there to be known, anyway? This is the central subject matter of *The Vivisector*: the ugliness, disjointed structure and elemental deformity of the human mind. The inability to find a pattern or even a sequence in the labyrinth of individual intentions that would construct the solid mandala for their existence – which White attributed to his other self. Or maybe it is only the mind of contemporary humans that is disjointed? Or only the social elites of Sydney? Or is it the confusion in the mind of Montaigne's *heedy reader*? Who can tell?

There is so much noise and not enough music around us today. We simply get addicted to its distractions. Complacency, easy satisfaction and an abundance of narcissistic reaffirmation makes us lose any sense of purpose, let alone of a centre, deterring us from exploring the meaning of happy failure and the premonition of transfiguration. And when we are confronted by books that decided to deal with this, we get scared and return to the warm protection of our addictions and prejudices – or to the suave conformism of our fragile and precious, sexual and ethnic identity.

The archetypal story of the fall in the mythology of many cultures, that humans fell from their primeval unity with the source, is reversed by White. His novels are about ascending from Hell to Heaven: humans are born in the gutter and look upward for redemption. They are born in Hell and, through suffering, ascend to their paradise. When they arrive there – *if* they arrive there – they simply lick their wounds and try to find some rest and sleep. *The there was always here*: confusing, beguiling and upsetting.

His characters start with nothing and in nothingness; through the total dismantling of their existence, the total deregulation of their senses, after being emptied of all their vital potentialities, they enter their ultimate paradise. What might this paradise be? Just about anything; from a forgotten myth to the simplest pleasure that homelessness and rejection can offer: *no rats ... and an easy pee... That's something, isn't it?* That's the end of *The Night the Prowler*, Jim Sharman's 1978 movie for which White wrote the screenplay, his ultimate confrontation with the pretensions of the bourgeoisie, the grandiloquence of nihilism and the alibis of modern smugness. In religious terms, it would be called kenosis – but the term itself opens up a new discussion which will makes us lose our way.

Language, yet again

Among the most important novels on artistic psychology in the last century, Broch's *The Death of Virgil*, Mann's *Doctor Faustus* (1947) and Somerset Maugham's *The Moon and Sixpence* (1919), *The Vivisector* stands out for the depiction of artistic creativity through its negative capabilities.

Writing begets something that goes beyond the adventure of individual life. White's work is an enigmatic repository of ethical questions. Whoever reads his novels is struck, not simply but the intricate plots or their paradoxical and quirky characterisations, but also by the ethical questions that we find illustrated and elaborated in them and occasionally through them. All of his novels deal with different ethical questions and struggle to answer them in terms of aesthetics. Such an approach opens up his texts to extremely complex perceptions and, at the same time, to highly intriguing and provocative formal geometries. How can we aestheticize ethics? Is it permissible? Is Wittgenstein's brave statement about ethics and aesthetics valid or, more importantly, true?

Furthermore, despite the deeply inquisitory character of his novels, this does not mean that answers are always given; White finds out that certain questions do not have a single answer; or they may not have any answer at all. They remain constantly re-defined and re-articulated according to the situation from which they emerge, bound by their specificity and uniqueness.

White deals with the indeterminate situations around problems, and less so with the answers to those problems. He wants to outgrow them (as Carl Gustav Jung put it) instead of trying to explore any possible answers, or even trying to solve them. We do not solve or answer problems: we simply reconcile ourselves with them. Most of his novels end abruptly, and somehow continue to exist in abeyance. He remains the only Australian writer who leaves his readers with uncomfortable dilemmas, abandoning them without any closure. His Duffield converses with Balzac's Master Frenhofer, the mad painter in the story "The

Unknown Masterpiece" (1831). And he meets the same end.

From Voss to Duffield, we observe a change in direction and orientation: the former looks outward, searches the land for something, the primal fear of being forgotten in a remote corner of earth in which all days are full of bitter farewells and frustrated ideals. The latter turns inward and searches for redemption in the creative act, which is also an act of destruction and self-loathing. They both find the icy death which they were looking for. Everything was inevitable and impenetrable. Nature or human nature: the more they search, the less they discover. The novel is the realm of beings, of beings at home in themselves, even when they have no home or self. White makes each character find its proper essence: the common denominator of meaning that survives all readers and readings, and continuously re-signifies itself beyond the circumstances of reception or the fashions of interpretation.

All these many years after initial publication, Voss is not a desperado or a megalomaniac, but someone whose identity escapes his own mind. Duffield is someone who wants to be someone else, by giving birth to himself through beauty. They are both lost in themselves because they cannot come to terms with themselves. Their story gives fragments and traces of a mental world of dreams, experiences and memories, from which only the reader can extract a pattern and probable significance. Through these traces, the reader must reconstruct the entire mental edifice by imagining an implied architecture of experience.

I remember the dream sequences in *Voss*, or the creative eruptions in *The Vivisector*. They are striking and terrible. The dreams that connect Laura and Voss, or the painting "Lantana Lovers under Moonfire", make human gazes ecstatic with horror and pity. In their own unique way, the writing of these novels inaugurated conversations with unpredictable respondents, conversations which never seem to end. They are, however, conversations we don't want to have: that is, from a libidinal point of view. Who wants to address the enigmas of the self, of goodness and love, all three deprived of their most powerful quality: to instil us with passions, illusions and myths?

Well, then, what can we do with Patrick White? We listen to his novels the way we listen to Arnold Schoenberg's or Igor Stravinsky's music, as the confluence and the consilience of disparate and dissonant tunes and melodies. Stravinsky claimed that music can be experienced as "a form of speculation in terms of sound and time." So, too, can the novel; it can be experienced as a speculative dialogue with our internal others trying to express what Stravinsky again called "a desire for quiescence in multiplicity."

The ethics beyond

Why were ethical problematics so important to White's work? Some scholars have suggested that this "strong ethical" questioning is due to his personal anomie, his sexual life, and the modes of presentation he chose to indicate his sexuality under conditions of repression and disguise. Others have avoided the question by talking about the "heavy" aestheticisation of his work or try to address it by reducing everything to biographical particulars. Until recently, the most obvious reading-trope of his work was based on the archetypal patterns employed by White in some of his novels, in order to elucidate similarities in diverse experiences. The most cynical readers point out posturing and pretence, or global cabals of a psycho-sexual nature.

According to During's unfortunate and exoteric study, White's novels were suspended in no-where and no-one's land, between the cultural industry and narcissistic self-mythologisation. He supposedly defended aesthetics in an age in which aesthetics are proven to be instruments of oppression and expressions of privilege. Even his mythopoetics indicate unconscious bias and patriarchal prejudices. During's study opened the can of worms which have, ever since, partially destroyed, for the mind of impressionable youths, the possibility of any informed and fair reading of White's novels – and probably, of all novels from the past. During, like most scholars of such

Quixotic kind, projects onto the books his own panics and dilemmas – indeed, some would claim, his own personal obsessions and demons, not to mention his professional interests, which he seems to find everywhere in White's novels.

During takes his own inability and failure to understand literature as the inability and failure of those who write literature to confirm his own expectations. His circular thinking, revolving around the vicious circle of omniscience, projects on the semiotic structures of White's novels the utilitarian ethics of contemporary, corporate capitalism – which, in a warped way, he interprets as a revolutionary project. Lacking in hermeneutical method, he is unable to see and experience the otherness of an artefact constructed by anyone other than himself.

Yet the question arising from this is larger and more pernicious. The cult and heresy of presentism has become the dominant method of un-imagining the past of literature, restricting everything to a superstitious cult of nowness sanctioned by the flippant canonisation offered by awards and the constant interviews with publicists and journalists. During sees literature as another industry, not as the space of collective identifications.

Certainly, literature is not about instilling ethical propositions: it problematises ethical conditions, but its function is not to tell us how to live or what to do. Its function to present through its dramatic myth, its mythopoeia, a meta-ethical language in which to study the consequences or the side-effects of the worldviews illustrated through the characters. Literature does not moralise; if it does, it ceases to please, since it wants to instruct. Like philosophy, it is the study of death but, most properly, of dying – and therefore gives readers reasons to live.

It is the difference in Tolstoy's works between *War and Peace* (1869) and *Resurrection* (1899). Literature explores the what-ifs of the human mind through plot and character. Trying to reduce everything to the contextual realities of a work's time simply mischaracterises the novel, particularly, as some sort of anti-Bible, a quasi-religious book which raises universalist, ethical imperatives. Yet a novel, even when it moralises – as many novels by Dostoevsky, Hermann Hesse or Iris Murdoch do – it does so to explore the limits of moral conditions, and problematise the limitations of ethical stipulations.

White's work illustrates an ethical exploration of human confusion, against the background of its own psychological complexity; as such, it avoids any structures of meaning which could be considered conclusive, therefore eliminating or reducing human agency and human initiative. In his novels, the reader can easily detect structures which look paradoxical or even self-contradictory.

White is one of the most confusing writers, in the sense that he deflects the expectation of his readers toward directions unpredicted by his narratives, or by the conventions of the novel. The main innovation of his verbal artistry is this *narrative deflection* that turns the attention of his readers away from an expected pattern of articulation into a quite grand, almost cosmic pattern of redemption – the design of which can be detected only in small details, disconnected episodes and partialised fragments. *The Solid Mandala* is precisely about this cosmic projection which the reader can perceive only through bits and pieces, the sticks and stones of words that the writer has put together. This point has nothing to do with archetypal readings which, having served their purpose, are totally misleading today.

If we may carry the metaphor further: through such narrative deflection, White attempts something more structural and comprehensive: semantic refraction. Most of his stories, characters and plays develop fields of signifying uncertainty, continuously pushing the potentialities of meaning to extreme liminal formations. The aesthetics of excess so persistently employed by White point toward this liminality: after a point, everything becomes an unsettling imponderable. *Youth is the only permanent state of mind*, he wrote. *If growing old is to become increasingly aware, as a little boy his premature awareness irritated his elders to the point of slapping. So there are in fact no compartments, unless in the world of vegetables.* Non sequiturs: White's central mode of articulation. This is how he wanted to populate the Great Australian Emptiness: with imaginative leaps of faith into overlooked spaces of living.

Yet no one can deny the fact that, through such uneasy aesthetic inventions, something specifically realistic, almost documentary emerges from his narratives. For years, following him, I had sardonically dismissed Leonie Kramer's observation that White's novels were *documenting* the real atmosphere of emotions and hardships experienced in Australia after the World War II. I wondered: how could a symbolic realist like White document anything?

Even though I worked at the same institution as Dame Leonie, we met only in airports. Sydney, Melbourne, Brisbane, Singapore, Beijing, even London. Waiting for our connecting flights. It was inevitable that we would talk about Patrick White, who shunned her so gracelessly in his memoirs. "He was a *prosateur*," she told me in Beijing, using Sartre's term. "Not a novelist. He tried to poeticise the prose of our society." Wow, she knew Sartre's theory of literature! I was a bit annoyed, because I had forgotten all Sartre's books I devoured in my youth. You read so much of Sartre, and you remember nothing: some titles and only the first line from *The Words*. But *prosateur*? From Dame Leonie? To this day, I cannot swallow it. That's one of my most detrimental personal failures.

The Aesthetic Imperative

However, in order to articulate his moral aporias, White had to re-configure the expressive and, especially, the performative function of language. Indeed, the main problematic which his work explores is that of the limits of language, and of the various ways in which language may articulate experience, especially experience which hasn't found its epiphany in language yet.

His novels can be seen as long, ethical studies: both ethical and ethicising explorations of the nature of human relations, dealing with the unexpected moral qualities that emerge through human interaction. As such, they address questions through a rather challenging, myth-making structure. White avoided the accepted 19th century representation of narrative time; despite the linear, somewhat traditional authorial omniscience of his novels, their linguistic form depicts a universe which is unstable and centreless, held together by uncertain, fragile patterns of evanescent transparency that link bodies, events and landscapes in a narrative pattern full of omissions and empty spaces. Indeed, what interests him is the *illusory character* of human identity, by exploring how meaningless hyperactivity obscures the possibility of human communication.

Historically, the main premise of White's writing is simple: after his return to Australia, he developed a more or less conscious project to emancipate the language of his surrounding artistic reality from the dominant forms of expression as found in the British writers of the period. Yet, as a writer of his time and society, White suffered from the trauma of emancipation – an emancipation which he longed for but, once achieved, left behind dark spots of negation and nostalgia. His novels are permeated by the sense of a missing unity, an absent centre, one could call it a patricidal murder, which renders his language so unfamiliar and yet so paradoxically accurate. How does one live as an adult, having been separated from the maternal authority of a hegemonic culture? What kind of relations can he establish with the lost beginning of being, when he understands that he must live with the guilt and anxiety of having left the centre that gave him birth, and yet forced him to discover his individuality? White's works are about such questions and their aesthetic form; he sees their form as the best pathway to existential reality, therefore as ethical studies which are left inconclusive because of the antinomic tension of their structure.

The writer pushes language to an almost anti-linguistic articulation, in order to bring something which is eluding beyond articulation to consciousness. White's novels are about the limits of the conscious self and the articulating patterns which can be established in order to locate and indicate the lived experience in them. The central premise that coheres White's novelistic project is his own, autobiographical statement: *The ideal Australia I visualised during my exile and which drew me back, was always, I realise, a landscape without figures.* His entire work, therefore, is about landscapes without figures, or displaced figures without landscapes; such an absence frames the quest for form in his writing. From the first pages in *The Tree of Man* to the last scenes of his play *Shepherd on the Rocks* (1987), White struggles to co-relate landscapes to human figures, places to actions, and essentially symbolic realities to forms of actual experience.

Furthermore, White's novels depict an immense *incommensurability* between the real human presence and the natural reality around them; the basic collision within his work is located in the polar opposition of nature versus culture. Throughout his work, the negative but numinous presence of nature became one of most dominant forms of articulating the collective experience of Australia.

Indeed, one could claim that White's work tries to establish an intelligible relationship between the human and the natural realm, which coexist in an uneasy ambivalence. This equivocation extends not simply to the historical dimension of the details during the exploration of the country. But the exploration theme becomes, in itself, a fused metaphor for the unknowability of the human mind, and its inability to establish meaningful patterns of communication.

From the beginning of the modernist movement with Joyce and Proust, the great dilemma concerned aesthetics and its connection with life. Indeed, both Proust and Joyce advanced aesthetic arguments close to the ethical realm of understanding, without crossing over to the ethical problematisation of the artistic act itself. They were both firm in their belief that the artist had a superior understanding of the enigmas of life and therefore great art had one mission: to decipher these enigmas for the ignorant and philistine bourgeois. White's work expresses, more than any other contemporary work, a unique problematisation of both the aesthetic and the ethical, depicting them in constant tension: in some works, the former wins and in others, the latter. Yet this tension was extremely useful to the writer in regard to his mythopoetic forms; in some of his early works, the aesthetic dimension was central for the self-understanding of the author and his narrative.

In the novels after *The Tree of Man*, however, White embarked on the most persistent and somewhat uneven attempt to explore the centreless realm of ethical decisions and conditions, in a way unparalleled to the history of Australian writing until then – and roughly equivalent to the great novelists of the late 19th and early 20th centuries in their mature work. Sometimes you think that he is conversing with George Eliot or Thomas Hardy, and at others with James Joyce and Virginia Woolf.

Contemporary scholarship tends to re-inscribe his works with problematics of identity, ethnicity, sexuality, gender or post-colonialism which were not visible within his own conceptual horizon. Certainly, this can be extremely fruitful – but it can also become anachronistic, diminishing the historical consciousness inscribed in the work. We cannot erase the dimensions of writing which were not only visible but also dominant in the way that White perceived the act of writing. Such differentiation will help us understand the qualitative and quantitative divergence between Balzac's *Séraphîta* (1834) and White's *The Twyborn Affair*. Androgyny in the former is a recreation of the original and unfallen nature of the soul whereas in the latter the dissection of the unstable identifications of contemporary gendered subjectivities.

The work of art is, in its very structure, intentional: especially in White's case, it was written in order to intensify and magnify forms of life and patterns of communication which were unvalidated by cultural codes and did not enjoy social visibility. Based on an open and often convoluted dialogue with dominant forms of articulation, White created a singular configuration and constructed a picture of this "illegitimate world." His novels can be seen as a continuous, cognitive map of the cultural otherness of such illegitimacy around him and, indeed, within him. One could claim that most of his works present studies of legitimation, while showing the depths and boundaries of the de-legitimation processes in human interaction.

Indeed, as I have earlier suggested, White's novels are grand narratives of exploration; explorations in mythmaking, in language articulation, and ultimately in ethical questioning. Each one of these is expressed though different notions, references and functions. And the *topos* of their convergence, the actual text, is made up of multi-dimensional, prismatic characteristics, crystallising both the certainties and the aporias in his writings. One of the most interesting characteristics of his writing is what may be termed as *density of vision*.

Many critics, starting with A.D. Hope, thought of White's density as the main anti-aesthetic element in his writing, an element that blurred the clear representation of the social world as seen in previous or contemporaneous Australian writers. Such criticism has been echoed by mainly British reviewers of his novels, who criticised their dislocated and irregular language, the strange use of punctuation and paradoxical forms of articulation. But, in the very density of his work, we can find

White's most interesting and most enduring significance.

White perceived the actual text not as the site of a romantic revelation, or the emergence of classical principles of order and harmony. In White's novels, we see the textual dimension of the irregular, the unpredicted and the anomalous. The entire aesthetic of his work is based on the complete demolition by the writer of every attempt to find coherence, regularity and linearity within language and experience. White is one of the most anti-deterministic of writers; he un-focuses language to such an extent that the complete text of his mature novels is based on unstable grammar and syntax, thus creating a rather peculiar referentiality.

White didn't aspire to create types, anti-types or prototypes of human behaviour; consequently, I see the archetypal Jungian interpretation of his work, which dominated its study for so long, as totally missing the point. Nor did he want to explore the dynamics of gender or trans-gender in a Freudian typology, for which he was so unfairly criticised by During.

Whoever reads White's novels immediately feels that his characters, his language, his sentences present something exceptionally de-centred, profoundly ec-cenctric and hyperbolic – in the literal sense, exorbitant. They have lost their centre and rush through space toward their own limits. Yet you feel that they are very close to you and your history. They are unusual, but they are your neighbours. And who is my neighbour? Definitely not anyone who looks like me. My neighbour is inhabiting an indeterminate temporality, which challenges and distracts me, but reminds me, all the same, of something in me which wanted to see and to be seen: this reconnects me with something primary and originary, the unveiled beingness of my existence.

There is a great poem by Dionysios Solomos, unfinished and fragmented just like everything else by the man who became Greece's national poet, which talks precisely about this. It is late night, the hero is in the middle of the sea, close to drowning. He hallucinates and, in the best romantic fashion, sees before his destruction a maiden "dressed-in-the-moon" emerging out of the strange fusion of tempest and darkness. Solomos gives us the verses that delineate the hermeneutics of recognition, of *anagnoresis*:

Methought I had seen her, way back in the past
Perhaps in a church painted by an artist unsurpassed,
Or deeply carved in my memory, by my passion led,
Or in a dream, when by my mother's milk I was fed;
It was a memory of old, sweet, and almost faded,
Now standing in front of me with its force unabated.

I have frequently recited these verses, especially when I read something new and unknown. In the strange ways that the unconscious knows to manifest itself, the reading of some of his works awakens in me the recollection of indelible primary experiences, and connects me with Stan Parker, Waldo, Hurtle Duffield and the composite figure made of fact and fiction, Mr Patrick White himself.

The same effect can be seen in the way that White deals with the way he employs language at the most skeletal level of construction. At first glance, there is a strange ambivalence on behalf of the writer toward his own characters. The reader cannot locate the focal point of White's entry into his own stories. It is not simply the fact that White lived in an era when the anti-hero or the negative hero were dominant, thanks to French existentialism. There is no Albert Camus, Jean-Paul Sartre or Claude Simon in his work, unless to be laughed at. White has the morbid tendency to create unsympathetic characters through which no empathic identification with the reader could ever take place. Most of his stories point toward contradictory emotions and map out a literary space in which the familiar becomes so concrete that it loses its mystery and becomes hopelessly trivialised.

This *trivialisation effect*, if we may call it that, intends to deconstruct the habitual reading expectations that a novel must create or use 'verisimilar' characters. White always spoke out against the "journalistic mode" in novel writing, as prevalent in Australia –together with novels about the never-ending perpetual passage to adolescence full of confused libidinal economies. Despite their vividness, powerful physiognomy and unforgettable peculiarities, most characters in his novels present something exceptionally un-orthodox: they always 'live' on the boundaries of social normality, of accepted literary qualities and of 'believable' characterisation. The pattern is repeated throughout White's work, so it must be deliberate and intentional. His characters grow-up quickly, and they have no time to experience the hormonal tribulations of characters whose greatest terror is the passage to adulthood.

What did you learn from 50 years of confessions? This is what André Malraux asked a priest. And the devastating answer was: there are no grown-ups. White writes novels for those who have decided to grow up and deal with the passage of time. There are no kidults or men-boys in his works, and all his women are ceremonial priestesses (even Mrs. Roxburgh in the *Fringe of Leaves*). In a culture that deliberately infantilises people, his novels are truly unreadable. Instead of insisting on the supposed tribulations of race, gender, sexuality and whatever other fad is dominant amongst critics, White knows that the main subject of all novels is the passage of time, in terms of bodily change, the certainty that you cannot enter the same rime twice, and that ultimately your body is the river whose flux you must translate into verbal rhythms and musical phrases. The novel confronts the reader with the limitations of their mortality: if death is our ultimate nature, what does your gender, skin and sexuality matter? Blake knew this when modernity began:

In Great Eternity, very particular form gives forth or emanates
Its own peculiar light, and the form is the Divine Vision,
And the light his garment. This is Jerusalem in every man
A tent and tabernacle of mutual forgiveness, male and female
clothing,
And Jerusalem is called Liberty among the children of Albion.

White's anthropological vision energises the sticks and stones of words, their constructive imperfectability. A complete landscape appears in front of me, the reader. Many writers have plains, houses, hills, rivers, mountains; White has landscapes, vast geographies, *anthropogeographies*, large expanses of outer and inner worlds, which also include a place for the reader. They are stories without plots, starting *in medias res* and ending *in medias res*. It is the monumentality, the *Gothic splendours* that seem to mesmerise and make us succumb to all the temptations of a writer who wants to change boundaries and expectations.

Refamiliarising

There is another element in White's work which puzzles and alienates: the structure of his sentences, the sequence of words, the texture of his paragraphs. His connectives, adverbs and conditionals create a sense of an almost Brechtian *Verfremdungseffekt*, which imposes an invisible barrier between the writer and his readers. White uses this unexpected form of de-familiarisation even in his most "sublime" moments, in *Voss* for example: the dream sequence, when the incredibly majestic dream of Laura feeding Voss lilies is gradually transformed into a repulsive and disgusting gluey plaster which makes him vomit. There are many examples of similar performative narratives, which a superficial reading would consider as mere exhibitionism. In *The Vivisector*, the constant juxtaposition of sublime artistic thoughts with excremental references is another example. Yet he knows that, in order to de-familiarise your readers from what you say, you must de-familiarise your writing from what it means.

White's practice is on both sides of the semantic divide: he distances the reader from the story and the story from the writer. He is everywhere and nowhere, no character actually represents him and his ideas: he is an alien in his own world – and he loves it. Very few writers managed to do this: *avant la lettre*, he deconstructed the basic dominant function of novelistic language, not in the way of William Faulkner or John Dos Passos, but by making the destructured text part of the textual reconstruction of meaning.

Beyond his opposition to the verisimilar, journalistic pattern of writing, the main quest in White's novels, from *The Tree of Man* to his autobiography, and even his last novel, is the intented attempt to reconstruct, establish and consolidate invisible figurations for an embodied continuity of life. Such figurations first reflected his own precarious position in a society in which he existed as a 'prodigal son', and within his own literary tradition as a marginal and peripheral case. His sexual life might have also contributed to his self-marginalisation within the English language of his day, but it was not as central as During has suggested.

From such a dual position, White was extremely privileged to be able to look at social and literary conditions with astounding clarity, and a somewhat demoralising sincerity. In a sense, White's work is a hybrid formation between Dostoevsky's transcendental criminal and Tolstoy's integrating moral universalism. To George Steiner's dilemma, Tolstoy or Dostoevsky, White answers: both.

Indeed, between these two writers – one living in historical chaos and dreaming of divine order, the other having expressed human order and descending into the abyss of the unknown God – we can locate White's colliding signifiers coming together in an uneasy symbiotic relationship. From their collision, White struggles to locate what I would call figurative connections: a "new literary continent" needed new mythic structures in order to articulate and bring out this newness. This is what D.H. Lawrence had discovered in the writers of the United States: the new themes that the American experience generated asked for novel ways to be expressed.

As Lawrence pointed out: "Never trust the teller, trust the tale." White is not in his stories. His spectacular absence makes his work so *prosopographic*: like in his mandala, the hidden face looks back with intensity and curiosity, but it is not the face of its fabulator. Someone else looks out through the pattern and the writing; readers feel deeply awkward sensing that someone is perving on them, without being able to avoid that piercing gaze.

One can see a deep existential dysphoria in White's work: a structural conflict between the language of his upbringing – hegemonic, patriarchal and violent – and the language of his private existence, polymorphous, heterogeneous and irregular. In most of his novels, White relocates the subject of writing by unfocusing narrative time from the usual forms of dramatic climax and diffusing them through ambiguities and atypicalities. Such unfocusing creates the sense of total confusion that we find in his very language, the forms of articulation and the configurations he employs in order to transpose his private experience onto the level of an integrating mythos.

Many critics found White's language self-indulgent and pretentious (we remember here the "illiterate verbal sludge" by A.D. Hope). I would rather call it *liminal*: it builds a cognitive map of his world from its borders, or from deep below, even from outside its provenance. White's language establishes an existential otherness within the provenance of the real, by employing syntax, grammar and typographical appearance in a fragmented seriality. The newness of the Australian experience brings out the reality of silence and *aphanisis* in White's work: something always vanishes in his novels – and what vanishes is the familiar and the domesticated. The main narrative strategy employed by White toward this is to make everything visible, palpable and ubiquitous and then evaporate it into thin air.

Yet the glorification of the visible that we find in his novels aspires to show the invisible shadows in between objects and beings: they depict the reality of the inter-objective and intersubjective space. The invisible protagonist of his novels is the empty space between humans and things; so, they are essentially about the fields of psychic energy developing in-between, the semantic energies that emerge through the osmosis of beingness happening when things and beings are juxtaposed and interact.

Through such osmosis, something else emerges which is uncharged with emotion or the body electric – something which his very language struggles to envelop and inhabit, but which is constantly deferred and displaced. For example, his taste for un-eroticised eroticism is of immense, Freudian importance. White's novels are focused on displaced, indeed misplaced, desires; they are based on the unsayability of emerging qualities of being which are beyond the provenance of language. So, the density of his work is an exploration of the potentialities of language to elucidate dimensions of experience not belonging to the linguistic realm.

Through the liminal language of tragic comedy, White expressed what his society was trying to repress; yet his work is an ironic resistance against repression. In that respect, and recalling André Malraux once more, his work created an *anti-destiny* for his society, something problematic and unsettling, through representational codes that were always off-centric, and could not be invested with the authority of a canonical work – unless de-temporalised or de-contextualised. Simon During's puerile study attempted a rude landing, as it were, on the gross terrain of the cultural industry, supposedly debunking all approaches to White's work as a quasi-religious or archetypal cypher. It brought us back to earth but failed, I believe, to show the topography of the world it was demolishing – and, as such, couldn't account for anything save the shock value of its ponderous platitudes.

Most of During's pronouncements are catchy captions in power-point presentations for first-year students, full of click-baiting buzzwords and wooden clichés, intended to amuse and befuddle thrill-seeking bourgeois readers. During read White's work as if it was written by Barbara Cartland – a writer to whom most of his conclusions seem to refer.

The presumed correspondence between life and work, and the implicit idea that, in one way or another, writers want to justify their lifestyle is, beyond any reasonable doubt, inaccurate or inapplicable to White's personal vision of the psyche. He was one of the very few writers who declared in all possible ways, implicit and explicit, that he didn't like many aspects of his own self and that there was something profoundly wrong in him which he himself couldn't ever accept and justify.

And this was not his sexuality, his social position or his privilege. Beyond all else, White felt dysphoria concerning his incomplete humanity, his broken self-perception, his sense of a superfluous existence.

In an era of smug self-importance and narcissism, this was brave and challenging. The dramatis personae in his books, from *The Aunt's Story* to *The Eye of the Storm*, want to be unlikeable, and thus betray their writer's relation to them: the inadequacies of their character are exacerbated by the precarious postulates of their morality. In Freudian terms, in White there is always an antagonistic relationship between ego and superego. In his development as a writer, he came into conflict with the Protestant Christianity that formed his mind, and the civil culture of possessive individualism that Protestantism constructed in the Western world. From this constant friction a personal, almost private, imaginative empathy evolved – a holistic tendency to justify and understand all forms of life. In his universe, moral freedom grants the right to be wrong. Being wrong doesn't mean being evil. As Socrates stated, no one is willingly bad. On the basis of such profound problematics, White anchors his empathy for characters he dislikes.

For the same reason, White avoided the theatrical nihilism of many post-WWII writers, like Beckett, Emil Cioran and Camus. Writing, and art in general, does not answer the enigma of death, or even assuage the fear of being-toward-death. Writing addresses the enigma of birth: it deals with the potentialities engendered and fertilised by our birth. What surprises in *Voss*, in particular, is the un-romantic and anti-melodramatic description of death: all deaths are simple and natural phenomena of living. The question has been formulated at the very beginning: why here? Why you? What for?

Ultimately, the central questions of White's *natalist aesthetics* are of a religious nature and have transcendental consequences. All aesthetics impose a gap between the real and its perception: this vacuum makes people feel that they are not there yet. They have to fill the chasm with their own creative effort, with their own *natality*. In all forms of art, the more we excoriate religion, the more it will come back, powerful and bewitching. White called this spirituality an invisible, divine presence which *controls us but to a certain degree* – and that degree of freedom is commensurate to the intensity of our creativity.

Some of his readers, coming from different traditions, wouldn't really understand the fiery pastors that we find in his pages, and probably focus on those crazy prophets in the social margins as found in *Riders in the Chariot* or the existentialist ruminations in *The Solid Mandala*. As Eastern Orthodox myself, I find Protestantism exceedingly un-Christian, idiolectic and therefore untheological; its quest for a singular and unalterable meaning totally deconstructs the theological foundations of language in Christianity.

Arnold Toynbee observed that Protestantism was the resurfacing of Judaism and Islam in Christian garb. By its monolingual hermeneutic, and by abolishing the experience of the mysterious and the uncanny, Protestantism brought back demonology as a counter-reality, and led to the demonisation of all differing ideas. Australian Protestantism, in particular, lacks a theology of contrition and humility, while wallowing in the narcissism of the Puritan battle-cry about us, "wretched sinners in the hands of an angry God". The idea that you will be perfect on earth as is your father in Heaven is probably the most hubristic and diabolical idea ever contrived by the human mind since the time of the Tower of Babel or Prometheus. Even the idea that God is angry indicates that for Protestants the New Testament has not been written yet, and that Jesus was simply a prophet of the Hebrew Bible.

In a way, it is the difference between Ingmar Bergman's *The Seventh Seal* in which the knight prays to God not to kill him for one more day, and Andrei Tarkovsky's *Nostalghia* (1983) where God himself reveals that he is everywhere – and yet the believer cannot see anything. I am afraid that these are problematics, indeed a set of questions, which cannot and never will enter the English language, bedevilled as it still is by the presence of evil in humans, unable to explore the goodness in them or try to reconstruct the "very good indeed" that the eyes of God saw after the sixth day.

Only Shakespeare managed to save the experience of English in English from the Babylonian captivity of nothingness. And as long as Shakespeare is, then mystery will crack the opaqueness of tradition. *Language is difficult. But a word will suddenly flash out, won't it Waldo? – for somebody who doesn't always understand.* White knew that the limits of his language were not the limits of experience: he dislocated language so that the underlying furious magma of goodness would gush out and complete the image.

The cornerstone of Anglican Protestantism is not the message of Jesus, but the sublime sentences of the King James Bible, with its demand for the avoidance of ambiguities. *Sola Scriptura*! Is it possible? It is bibliolatry and biblicism focused on the written revelation which inferiorises the visible creation, which is the first and ultimate revelation – and that's White's ultimate religion and faith. The King James text and its semantics still reign supreme; they embody and impose their own theology and doctrines. Many writers understood the problem. Thomas Hardy, George Eliot, Maugham, Aldous Huxley, even Graham Greene, looked elsewhere for the theology of the real and its ensuing anthropology. *Religion,* White said. *Yes, that's behind all my books. What I am interested in is the relationship between the blundering human being and God.* And then he had to deal with the God issue: how to deal, therefore, with the unsayable and the unrepresentable? Since God speaks in un-linguistic manifestations, the writer has to fill the gaps.

White tried to ambiguate his stories, to infuse them with the polysemic references of non-verbal languages – in *The Vivisector* particularly, the language of colours. The visible revelation takes precedence over the limits and limitations of a culturally bound text. Human history in the Bible begins with the confounding of tongues after Babel, and restarts with the violent wind of the Pentecost, when everyone could hear their own language being spoken. White's novels are Pentecostal: they declare the wonders of existence polyphonically and at the same time explore the amazement and the awe of those who witness these wonders.

His ambiguation led to a mystical perception of the divine as *the same mysterious universal Presence ignored, cursed, derided, or intermittently worshipped by the human race*, as he wrote toward the end of his life. This is the numinous presence experienced by mystics, not the rational faith of believers. You can be a total atheist and yet accept the god of Spinoza, Einstein and Whitehead.

Milan Kundera in his short admirable book on the art of the novel pointed out Heidegger's "beautiful and almost magical phrase 'the forgetting of being'" – something which, he claimed, the novel was destined to abolish. These are the usual operatic exaggerations of *Mitteleuropa*. You cannot forget the being, or the *Seyn*, if you are surrounded by so many beings. They are too tangible, complex and incomprehensible to be reduced to a singular entity beyond language, an entity either veiled or forgotten. Beings are unpredictable, hence they don't fit any plot; they are contradictory, hence they cannot produce a philosophy; they are fallible, hence they dedicate themselves to fantasies and illusions. Kundera wrote also that "the novel is one of the last outposts where man can still maintain connections with life in its entirety."

For White, the ideal Sydney is the Neoplatonic suburb of Sarsaparilla – unreal, surreal and hyperreal, with all its characters lost in the mists of their own history. There is no way you can find a pattern of any interpretation for their existence. They exacerbate the chaotic nature of experience and map out a space full of pre-linguistic energy or post-linguistic angst. All is messy in this suburb because all is full of gods and demons. What are humans doing in the land of gods? They are outcasts and exiles. But they have no other place to call home. The Elysium of suburban bliss is their damnation. The paradise of bourgeois self-admiration is their eternal punishment. And the clash between humans and demons goes on fiercely at the protestant Walhalla. The novelist records the clash, knowing that there can be no resolution. The novel offers a temporary reprieve, a snapshot as it were of the rare moment of self-reflection. In a strange way, White followed Italo Calvino's suggestion that "the true novel lives in the dimension of history, not geography: it's human adventure in time, and the places – the places as precise and beloved as possible – are necessary as concrete images of time." Sarsaparilla, like Faulkner's Yoknapatawpha County, is the imaginary and apocryphal land in our midst where all cosmic battles take place today. Not in the mountains of madness or in the salons of the high aristocracy but in the flat land of unfulfilled dreams and broken promises. The home they struggled so hard to buy becomes their prison and their Calvary. Mrs Docker will never escape not even as a guest; she reminds everyone the open horizon in a landscape of lost horizons.

The Grammar of Sinsuality

The topography of White's novels resembles a grammar of temporal disclosures: anomalous and irregular, numinous and cryptic at the same time, full of evasions and revisions, full of exceptions. It illustrates a reality beyond the significations of decipherable codes, the uncomfortable reality of codes privatised by necessity – which, for some quirky twist of historical cunning, were invested with the aura of the cultural icon. Certainly, the language of Stan Parker is not the same as the language of Eddie/Eudoxia Twyborn: it is a matter of tone and velocity. Stan's language is fused and metaphoric; that of Eddie, inquisitive and assertive; Alf Dubbo's, mythical and chromatic. Yet they are all incomplete, arcane and fragmented. I remember here how Thomas Mann spoke about his novels as "dealing in dialectics, always letting the one speaking at the time be right." I always thought of *The Magic Mountain* when I read *Riders in the Chariot* and of *Dr Faustus* when I was reading *The Vivisector*. When they speak all their characters are right, and they are right because they were given the privilege to exist.

However, the lacunae in them all are too obvious to be hidden under the glory of opulent sentences: they frame a perspective that depicts the real in its ineffable specificity – and, at the same time, the terror in front of a possible unveiling of being in its terrible completeness. For a long period of time, it was hard (and generally undesirable) to confront our own self and fight against our own formation. How can anyone confront, ridicule or disgrace the most sacred moment of our existence, the only paradise they ever inhabited: our own childhood? Irony, parody and cynicism are all strategies to avoid the acidity of such inner conflict: innocence and guilt appear frequently in White's novels. But how?

In our post-postmodern world, we have accepted a world of fluid events beyond concrete representation, whereas in a world of symbols, the most challenging and pragmatic event is their very materiality, specificity and persistence. You cannot avoid symbols: they are the only reality we experience because they build relations, or correspondences. Yet not all symbols have representations. They are and remain diffused *numens*, which the writer struggles to name and readers to attune themselves with. Australia, for example, the city, the weather, nature as an all-embracing presence, and, of course, god, which ultimately becomes a colour: *All his life he had been reaching towards the vertiginous blue, without truly visualising, till lying on the pavement he was dazzled not so much but a colour as a long-standing secret relationship.*

The event of the phenomenological presence of a reality beyond representation is probably the most enigmatic aspect of White's writing. Proust adopted a prismatic approach to the real, by depicting it through as many surfaces as possible. In Proust's involuntary memory, there are many surfaces, but one single angle: the sick narrator who remembers and reassembles and doesn't quite distinguish if he is the boy going to bed early or the asthmatic sick man who will soon die.

White has no real central characters in his novels; they are all central to the drama of the narrative flow. *I always think of my novels as being the lives of the characters.* He qualified this: *All the characters in my books are myself, but they are a kind of disguise.* There are no plots or stories, he explained. There are only characters: not in the usual conventions of realism or the lifelike duplication of existing forms. But 'fresh forms' which spring from the unconscious suggest what he called the *illuminating experience*. Innocence and guilt is about the presence or the absence of such an experience not ethical laws or social perceptions.

Writing is based on the dissimilarity between reader and writer: if one reads books simply to discover copies of oneself or validation of one's own experiences, then there is definitely a cognitive dissonance in place. Just as cinema asks for suspension of disbelief, literature asks of suspension of all belief, especially of your beliefs. Flaubert allegedly said *Madame Bovary c'est moi*, but it is so untrue: all his readers know that it is untrue. Was Tolstoy Anna Karenina? Or Dostoevsky Alyosha Karamazov? Yourcenar more accurately said that Hadrian was her brother – which is always more likely in literary inventions. Literary characters are our soulmates, brothers and sisters in arms. With us, but not us. We discover them as much as they discover us. We are in the middle of an endless field, thinking that we are alone. Suddenly we look around and see that Kundera's Ludvik Jahn is next to us while making a silly joke; and that Marilynne Robinson's pastor John Ames (in *Gilead*), before his death, feels gratitude and is forgiven, because he gave forgiveness. And definitely, Ulrich Voss, helping us to live our myth so that *it will be written down, eventually, by those who have been troubled by it.* Each character is a portal not a field of identifications. It takes us elsewhere, where we have never gone by ourself – and that elsewhere matters in literature.

In the end, we all move on to a new order of being: from experience to memory, from memory to recollection, from recollection to bibliographical footnotes. And the ritual is repeated. But they are not you: if you identify with them, you simply project your dilemmas onto them, making them comment on the dramas of your frustration. Unfortunately, you are who you are, and you can do nothing more than be who you are. White is one of the most distinct and personal writers does not have an identity problem. Contemporary writers cannot really deal with the supreme truth of their being: *You're in the end–just what you are!/ Put wigs on with a million locks / And put your foot on ell-high socks, / You still remain just what you are.*

Identification as performance is probably the worst form of self-delusion that the publishing industry has imposed upon writers. It has also been trumped up by certain philosophisers without philosophy. Slavoj Žižek and Judith Butler come to mind as two thinkers of identity drowning in their own thought of specular impossibilities. With them, the transition from the spectacular self to the specular type, the virtual ghost self of post-modernity, is consummated. Cynical nihilism becomes the dominant thinking mood – and that's what the novel is fighting against: the derealisation of the senses, the loss of materiality in all things captured by our senses.

As readers, exposed to so many characters, but having to deal with our own self, we know that the greatest failure of imagination will be to identify with any character. Werther is no more, just as Hamlet and Gatsby and Frederic Henry (*A Farewell to Arms*) are no more. Their names delineate the limits of our being and force us to find our centre, in opposition to ourselves, and concretise our existence, stop being seduced by the lure of narcissism and projection. Voss compels us to find who we are by portraying what we cannot become.

Many have accused White of his misanthropy and his fallings out with so many people. The *Letters* (1995) overflow with numerous expulsions from friendship and proximity. Yet the novels are full of democratic absurdity and drollness: most dislikeable characters are involved in such surreal situations that readers do not really understand how they got there. A certain empathy is born, which makes them somehow funny and interesting. In White, Beckett meets Groucho Marx – and both fuse in an Elizabethan tragedy. Christopher Marlowe and Shakespeare, Edward II and Prospero, demonic mania and philosophical serenity. Yet, after so much strife, the *conjunction oppositorum* never happens: the tension retains its force, unabashed and unabated. This tension culminates in intimations of immortality, but only intimations. White knows when and where to pause; he drops some hints, and then the narrator vanishes.

Such festive absurdity becomes obvious in his late novels; until the rediscovery of natural sensuality in *A Fringe of Leaves*, his narrative structures frame the urban sprawl at its ablest and most astonishing polyphony. (His plays amplify the quest for the quirky and odd, the living irregularity that leads to unexpected existential breakdowns and breakthroughs.) To concretise the ineffable as ineffable within the complexities of modern cultures: this became the most permanent quest in White's late work; and, although his writing is firmly grounded in the society around him, in a way it is not context-laden as is the writing of Waugh, Naipaul, Ngũgĩ wa Thiong'o, or even Margaret Atwood, Orhan Pamuk, Coetzee and David Foster Wallace.

There is a strange fluctuation in the construction of the narrative voices and their signifiers.

Like Proust, he uses all his imaginative power to compose a book and "then erase unduly apparent traces of composition." Hence, there is an awkward temporality in the structural pattern of the sentence, as if, on many occasions, the narrator diverges from the author and a *third voice* emerges which belongs to neither of them. There is always someone else's tonality that inserts itself into the narrative lines of his novels. Whose vocal tone? That is probably an unanswerable question.

White expressed the real as a post-linguistic or pre-linguistic event, employing language in ways that depict the dark chasms of thinking. Episodes in many novels are beyond comprehension or justification: the rhododendron scene in *The Vivisector*, for example, or the poetry of Le Mesurier in *Voss*. They have no real function in the story. Through these episodes, the writer expresses his aporia and impasse in front of the puzzling complexity of his own characters and frames his story in such a way as to show that the figures within the landscape articulate questions beyond the landscape itself.

The entire work of White has therefore to be seen as addressing a series of aporias questioning temporality, consciousness, language and history– to the extent that they can find an answer within the framework of imploding modernity and the context of hyper-real postmodernity. What is challenging in White is his unabashed claim to universalism. This doesn't mean that he always achieves it; but the *The Tree of Man*, *Voss* and *The Vivisector* are enough. There, he attuned himself to the grand tradition of Cervantes, Rabelais and Tolstoy.

Our contemporary obsession with gender identity is an aspect that can both enlighten and obscure his work. His homosexuality can be problematic as all sexuality can be problematic (as we see in Tolstoy's *Anna Karenina* and in so many other works). The education of the senses, especially for writers, is not focused simply on their sexual life but, more importantly, on their ability to present the sexual experience with and of others – experiences that are othering them and bring out the other in them (and in us, the readers).

The complexity of White's stories is that, from the perspective of homosexual desire, they address experiences that anyone could have. His language made homosexuality a natural and plausible manifestation of the quest for meaning –and sometimes for meaninglessness. All sexualities are about yearning: they reveal our need for someone beyond us, and remain mostly without closure. All sexualities are about fantasies that will never be experienced. Until they are, and then they become embodied reality.

White knew that no sexual behaviour or identity is an altogether happy or satisfactory affair. There are so many cracks in human sexuality, so many uncertainties or underground corridors, that no one can ever be happy. Edgar Allan Poe knew that all too well, Emily Dickinson knew it too, but also Goethe and Tolstoy and, above all, Hemingway. Sexuality is never felicitous. And in most occasions, sex itself is frustrating and disastrous. Even the grand lovers of French literature, a tradition marred by *l'amour* from Laclos to Mauriac and from Zola to Marguerite

Duras, do not want to admit that love, sex, lust – whatever they call it – is not an experience that fulfils the human thirst for realisation, transcendence or sheer pleasure.

Even Michel Foucault, the most anti-sexual, failed novelist amongst the French dilletante, wrote the most obnoxious pages on sexuality: he never enjoyed it. It was like a dramatic role to him, sometimes tragic, sometimes droll – and always messy. They are all consumed and destroyed by desire: inspired and lost at the same time, homo or hetero or anything else beyond (or within) binaries; the erotic unsettles and causes panic. Jean Genet, Françoise Sagan, or indeed Gombrowicz and even Kundera are framed by the *l'insoutenable légèreté de l'être* because they cannot reconcile themselves with their own needs – or, more importantly, their own responsibilities.

White is one of the very few writers who admits that there are aspects in his personality of which he didn't himself approve. No work of his is an exercise in self-justification. Sometimes it is quite the contrary: it can give the wrong impression of masochistic torture which, to some Freudian hardliners, could be an exercise in self-admiration. But no; it is not that. White genuinely seemed to dislike aspects of his own self, in a form of existential renunciation of their reality. He wanted to be otherwise. He felt the incompleteness of his psyche: unintegrated and chaotic, yet unconsciously in love with its own inconclusiveness. And that's *human, all too human*, as Nietzsche said. The usual reality of great lovers was expressed by Catullus: *Ōdī et amō. Quārē id faciam fortasse requīris. / Nesciō, sed fierī sentiō et excrucior.* The perennial wisdom of Latin in all its magnificent display. Only outside your own language can you discover the truth of your language.

Through such splitting of the self, by the self, we can detect the foundational self that writes itself in White's novels. But sexuality is not enough to make someone interesting. It is generally unconceptualisable: only when it becomes embodied in someone who is not our ideal self, but a completely different person – only then does it regain its vital potency. The rest constitutes approximations or subterfuges. Displaced energies, according to Freud. And White's novels are about these energies, only because White knew the self-presence of the individual that made sexuality conceivable. More about that at the end of this diatribe.

In *The Vivisector*, White scrupulously analysed the inextricable connection between meaning and its opposite – which is not meaninglessness but confusion or, indeed, despair. And at the same time, he pointed to the formlessness of contemporary art which abolished all practices that led to the emergence of what was called beauty in the past. In opposition to the clichés of existentialism, White thought that even the absurd had its place in life and imagination; even the absurd can be beautiful and not simply provocative or subversive. *Everything that exists asks for its own crucifixion*, as a Byzantine mystic wrote. It therefore prepares itself for redemption and grace. Even the trite and ugly, the mundane and insignificant, the sly smile and sophisticated irony – all point to their own redemption, and the redemption of their reader in

White's novels. Dostoevsky had stated: *Everything that is true and beautiful is always full of forgiveness.* Or as White stated: *Perhaps true knowledge only comes of death by torture in the country of the mind.*

White's authorial approach is anchored in letting-go and, through this perspective, it can detect beauty and truth in blasphemy and morbidity. Another Russian writer wrote, in a lecture on Kafka's "The Metamorphosis", the only sentence that could save his total work: *Beauty plus pity – that is the closest we can get to a definition of art. Where there is beauty there is pity for the simple reason that beauty must die: beauty always dies, the manner dies with the matter, the world dies with the individual.* I never expected Vladimir Nabokov to be able to articulate such a statement. As a matter of fact, I refuse to believe that he did. It is stolen from *The Vivisector.*

Excursus

In 1978, Brett Whiteley won the Archibald Prize for his confronting painting, *Art, Life and the other thing*, one of the most terrifying paintings ever made. Whiteley's triptych should have been on the front cover of *The Vivisector*. The first panel, top right, is a cheeky photograph of the artist as a young idiot, irreverent and mundane at the same time. The second, in the centre, depicts the same face distorted and disfigured in a state of direct exposure to William Dobell's portrait of Joshua Smith from 1943. The gradual descent into disfiguration (bottom left panel) predominantly means a loss of form, the destruction of the morphogenetic fields of experience. In this last panel, the hand of God gives the deformed junkie – probably the painter himself, who is now a prehuman, or posthuman, baboon – a heroin syringe, as if it is the salvation and redemption from pain and destruction. The personal inferno of the painter becomes an extraordinary depiction of formal de-creation, which is probably the true name of Hell. A dehumanised existence also means a natural reality without humans: serene, pristine and pure, yet locked in the mystery of the fifth day.

When I saw the painting, I felt the same shivering and dread as when I first encountered Goya's painting *Saturn Devouring His Son*, one rainy night at the University of Athens on the 6th of December of the year of the Lord nineteen seventy-eight. I was in the first year of my studies, I was lost, I felt like a cosmic orphan (yes yes the usual problems, distant father, adoring mother, sexuality confusion, blah blah blah and, of course, Michel Foucault). I can still recollect what was happening around me, that evening, the weather, the city traffic, the faces of passers-by, the lights, the smoke, the shops, the lecture theatre, the seats and the faces of fellow students, so many centuries later. I can still recollect the shape of the clouds in the sky, their colour at sunset, the wet footpaths of Athens, the bookseller who sold me Georg Lukács' *The Destruction of Reason* and Lenin's *State and Revolution* for five drachmas each, the hair colour of a woman smoking heavy Gauloise, the breathing of students around me, the sound of the slide projector, the tortuous passage from Géricault to Delacroix to Goya and, above all, Professor

Chrysanthos Christou, who liked having classes after eight at night in winter, talking about that "*par excellence* Freudian painting, *avant la lettre*" in his words. It took me ages to decipher his accent. "*C'est votre père que vous voyer ici.*" He always spoke in French when he wanted to terrorise his students.

I was late, and I opened the door to the lecture theatre just before the enormous slide with Goya's *Saturn* came up. I was mesmerised, transfixed, frozen. I stopped in front of the big screen and looked with awe and horror. It was I who was devoured by his father. The professor's voice insisted: "*C'est votre père que vous voyer ici.*" I stood there hardly breathing, as the dread of the inexplicable suddenly emerged with Goya, Saturn, and probably the Professor himself. This happened in 1978, December six, St Nicholas Day. I remember this day vividly and involuntarily.

That sensation and its atmosphere never left me. When I encountered the real painting in Madrid, I was almost 30, unhinged, stupid and uncontrollable: yet, as I approached, my knees were trembling, my stomach was punched by an invisible fist, my hands were shaking. I couldn't speak and my eyes were transfixed on the painting in a hypnotic stupor. It's more terrible than I imagined, I whispered. I stayed in front of the painting for hours: time was suspended, there was nobody around me, absolute silence, and a thick cloud of blackness, as I relived the moment of my birth.

Decades down the track, I felt the same at the Art Gallery of New South Wales when Whiteley's painting confronted my semi-unconscious horror of deformation and disfigurement. I went to the gift shop to buy postcards and, as I wandered further, I heard a voice calling me: *Come and See.* That was a moment of epiphany, of evil epiphany. As if in a trance, I turned the corner to the Australian section, searching with my eyes for the source of that beguiling voice; and there it was in front of me. I spaced out, I surrendered, I felt paralysed. Immediately and unconditionally. The painting called me in. The bland colours left the frames and spilled all over the room: I was walking on those strange earthy colours, the browns, the oranges, the ochres, the strange yellows, the vast *peinture* before the painting. The face of the baboon and his pierced, chained hands pointed to the extreme suffering, the Passion, the imperilled soul, the soul lost. This body had suffered profusely. It was still suffering. It was permanently scarred, indelibly marked. It was mutating, going back in time, reconnecting with the animal and reptilian world. It had lost its *humanitas*, its history, its biography. In a way, the painting in its three parts re-membered a lost story. It re-assembled what remained ultimately unconnected; yes, there was a sequence but the connection from the smiling face of the first panel to the last was rather a broken mosaic of ruptures and chasms. What led to the deformities and the utter hopelessness of the other two? The inability of the soul to find its centre. To accept its flesh. To become the word and the image. The loss opened the mind to the numinous otherness of reality though self-destruction. The world was full and full-on, but the human body was cosmic driftwood, pulverised and rejected, yet ready to receive the gift and become fertile through the stench of decomposition.

Freedom and death: freedom is death. You can be free only after you forget your freedom and surrender your existence to a greater force, a virtue or a vice, that will destroy you. This happened in 1998, December six, St Nicholas Day. I remember vividly and involuntarily that day.

Back on track again

After seeing Whitley's painting, I paused and reflected. As our old friend William Wordsworth once wrote once: All genuine poetry takes its origin from emotion recollected in tranquillity. Ah, I whispered, this is *The Vivisector*, this is Hurtle Duffield. Morbid, sinister and upsetting nightmares – all recollected in tranquillity. I closed my eyes and remembered the Aegean Sea, the solar phenomenology of the unredeemable world, the parasitic beauty of the unexamined life – that's the world I am coming from. There are no nightmares in the Mediterranean. Only wonder and magic.

And the God, oh that God, knows how to forgive and absolve, how to console and heal. Ah, *The Vivisector*, I whispered again. It's a Protestant's paradise. Its birthplace is Valhalla, the underworld of the slain, filled with woes and demons. Hurtle Duffield, there is your home and your being. And you simply are a pawn on the chessboard of an insidious mastermind.

God the ruthless, relentless vivisector of all, the prototype of all assassins, the common denominator of beings, the Logos before the *let it be* was spoken – the wolf that devours humans and animals, and their bones, as Nikos Kazantzakis would have said. Or as Thomas Hardy declared: *'Justice' was done and the President of the Immortals (in Aeschylean phrase) had ended his sport with Tess.* We are all the sport of the President of the Immortals. He doesn't care for the outcome: he just likes playing with us. The divine is always insidious and troublemaking. Herodotus, the first novelist, knew that. *Phthonos theon*, the resentment of Gods for the successes of humanity, their hostility for the mere existence of humans, their envy for the creature that dares to emulate them, is the ultimate locomotive of history. The paradox of a God that gives life and the same God that takes it away creates the great abyss out of which all formal thinking emerges. All art addresses this devastating paradox; if it doesn't, it is trivialising journalism and verbal bewitchment. What makes us strong, however, also makes us weak – it's only a matter of time.

White explored the real as if it were hyper-real. And, consequently, the amoral as if it were a moral fable. He trusted imagination in his attempt to discover reality. *Imagining the real* is one of his most vicious attacks against all forms of realism, all forms of self-justifying naturalism – although we can clearly see the best pages of Émile Zola's *The Masterpiece* (1886) in some of his works. White truthfully wrote that realism became a misleading category for the framing of his work and ideas. Because of his truthfulness, he did find the real and transcended its terror; he avoided the heresy of what he called *journalistic prose*.

In *The Vivisector*, he used the most unmediated and raw language to which we can ever have access.

The language of *Das Es*, of the It, the pre-linguistic unconscious: fluid, anarchic and confronting. He did so because he created a moment *in which dreams and facts had locked in an architecture which did not appear alterable.* For this reason, he took a deep look into the human psyche, where he discovered its inability to revolt against its own principles and desires. *My power is made perfect in weakness.* These strange words heard by Paul indicating the *essential powerlessness* of human existence when confronting its own humanity, are diffused throughout all White's writings. We all stand below our own expectations: we voluntarily betray them and, if we don't find a solid mandala, our life becomes centreless and without horizon.

Nobody is consciously bad, said Socrates. It is so true and so hard to accept. At the moment Hurtle realises that there is something *defective* in his art. Something missing which is precisely what of himself is in his art and probably its best element. His art will undo him. It doesn't need him. He is peripheral, almost a detail, because *There were the paintings; but fortunately there was also painting: the physical act which rejuvenated and purified when he and nameless others were at their most corrupt*. Corrupt here means weak, fragile, helpless. Painting emptied him from all his *élan vital*: he surrendered to the terror of the real and redeemed himself. As Etel Adnan stated: I write what I see. I paint what I am. Seeing what I am is the great challenge in the *Vivisector*. Duffield is the final and ultimate Dorian Gray.

Can anyone find their spiritual self-justification through corruption? Maybe, yes, quite likely: can the "evil painting" relieve the anguish of being your own self? Or indeed Hurtle's hidden 'God paintings?' reveal the death of god? Maybe, yes, or indeed quite likely. As old Heraclitus said: *ethos anthopo daimon*, our character is our demon. When you realise that Lucifer is in you, and you have succumbed to all three temptations, there is nothing else to do but rethink and reconsider the unfulfilled, the unattainable, the colour beyond all colours: *all his life he had been reaching towards this vertiginous blue without truly visualising, till lying on the pavement he was dazzled not so much by a colour as a longstanding secret relationship. Now he was again acknowledging with all the strength of his live hand the otherwise unnameable I-N-D-I-G-O.*

Ultimately, White's works become more Wisdom literature, and less of a documentary *écriture* searching for its own centre, and yet always managing to find nothing except new ways to fail, collapse and vanish. *Others fashion man*, wrote Montaigne. *I relate him. I describe not the essence but the passage*. Unmissable parallel here: not the essence but the passage, the flow that cannot be entered, not even once.

Sometimes critics think that, behind such morbidity and cynicism, lies the tragic humanity of Thomas Hobbes. It seems untrue to me, but I am not really sure, nothing can be said with certainty, because you have to be really reserved with mystics. I find White closer to Kierkegaard: determined to be passionately wrong than insipidly right. White was not interested in making readers feel comfortable with the act of reading novels. Conformism was, and still is, the unsurpassed horizon of meaning for the Anglosphere: Evelyn

Waugh and Kingsley Amis who write like high-minded toffs, carefully and painfully hiding the proletarian boy in them. They want to be *nice*, because they want to be accepted. Whoever reads White's novels without pretension discovers his all too un-mystical vision of *transubstantiating deficiencies*. His characters have no ideal self. They cannot be perfect. They are full of flaws. They are afraid of being themselves. They are aware of the unsurpassable horizon of their fallibility. They will repeat endlessly the original transgression. They are ontologically sinful and existentially sinless – or maybe the other way around. But there they stand. They cannot do otherwise.

In White's sinners, however, there is a beguiling innocence while, amongst his righteous, there prevails a debasing malice. A vice can become a method of purification; and a virtue, a method for perdition. This can be mostly seen in his plays. In all of them, the expectations of viewers are frustrated and disenchanted. Unwillingly, the bad perform good deeds -and vice versa. Characters like Voss, Mordecai Himmelfarb, Alf Dubbo, the

Hunters, and so on, are looking for an escape from the prison of their mind, without being able to receive or find grace. *Illumination is synonymous with blinding*. The flame that brings light is also the fire that burns and obliterates.

The world around Hurtle is the empty space of Nietzsche after the murder of God. Its inhabitants try to kill each other in acts that can only make them feel the pre-sacrificial void acutely and aesthetically. But they cannot keep living in premonition. Aesthetics are not enough to make them exist in a world of tragic adventures. Yet the characters are not evil enough, or at least not sufficiently good at being malicious. Even when they fail to be good, their unconscious goodness prevails against their own will. So, they survive through their mutual dependence on dread, anxiety and fear. They collapse, remain broken and traumatised; but small acts of kindness and consideration make them feel that there is meaning in all this, some other dimension, another horizon in all lost causes and all time lost. Chekhov reigns here – Chekhov again, not Tolstoy. The gentle and humble doctor, not the wild, haughty moralist. He explored the *sin of goodness*, which is really why many 'criticasters' cannot forgive him. And so was White superimposing what he called the *irony of honesty*? This is the only way that *he would make the best of this cell in which he had been locked.*

It is true that sometimes, White's writing becomes excessive, titanic, almost satanic. As I grow old, I feel scared by the dazzling chromaticism of Hurtle Duffield, and humbly return to the Swedenborgian correspondences of Stan Parker, the prophetic pregnancy of the lonely and the humble. Stan Parker has the innocence of a prelapsarian existence: he doesn't really know if that God of his in the *gob of spittle* comes from the demiurge or the real deity. He stays on one side of the fence, unable to jump over and confront both sides of existence. He is reticent, but not evasive: neither expression nor communication is the question for him. Only presence.

Stan Parker is White's archetypal character, devised early in his life. He is an atmosphere. He is a promise and a horizon. Voss is its ultimate antithesis; rather amusingly tragic, unable to make a step back and confront the mixture of grandeur and egotism that forms his mind. Hurtle Duffield is the final apocalypse: *the desert didn't flower, but thorns sprang up in celebration of their victory*. His impurity liberates the reader from the need of closure. Human autonomy has its cost. The vivisector cuts through your mind and dissolves your body. Only the paintings survive the existential demise.

And who, anyway, is the real vivisector? *Deus sive natura*? Are nature and God interchangeable? Or, as with any transcendentalism, is it the mental ability to think of the inconceivable and unexperienced presences that transform the real into a potential *Heilige Geschichte*? The numen in his paintings? Probably yes: *the tables and chairs now appeared the most honest works he had ever conceived, and probably for that reason the most nearly nouminous*. Image is psyche, stated Jung. Only images matter. I wanted to avoid Jung when talking about White, but there you go. I feel trapped.

White the novelist is always on guard to tell readers that there is something to be known. He is the writer of perpetual presence. Through the mythopoetic convergence of many disparate, interconnected narratives one can become part of the unifying experience of reading. This is an unintended consequence of the mythopoetic *geist*: even if it is pessimistic and inchoate as in the works of Ernst Junger or Curzio Malaparte, or jocular and sentimental as in W.M. Thackeray or Evelyn Waugh, the novel is the periscope of memory that salvages phenomena from oblivion. Some novelists tend to focus on the conflict of narratives, and others on their connectivity. Kundera has spoken valiantly on this issue.

Patrick White makes us conscious of those elements common in all narratives from all ends of town and all walks of life. His presumed anti-humanist cynicism is a protest against the inability to recognise the complexity of life and the multiplicity of beings. Yet he knows: all subjectivities exist in the pursuit of a shared narrative: they are motivated by the nostalgia for a *communitas* which they may have not experienced but feel that it exists somewhere in the realm that brings us all together – the omnipotent loom of language that weaves shared stories even against the will of those who tell them. The problematic heroes of modernity still bear in them the residues of the grand individuals we find in Homer and Vergil. The novel never forgets its roots and the novelists their patron saints.

All interconnected stories are about the most singular and unique theme, especially after modernity and (even more so) post-modernity. White encapsulated it already in his *The Aunt's Story*: *We must destroy everything, everything, even ourselves. Then at last when there is nothing, perhaps we shall live.* All his novels are about symbolic self-destruction: the author, the narrator, the narrated self, the myth, the story. They must all be destroyed, because they are all defeated by their own vision. This is a theme, a mythos, unique in the work of White: it cannot be recycled like Fitzgerald's Gatsby or Hemingway's Santiago. The only purpose of reading is to offer the *consolation of prose*. The vision within the art-work makes language meaningful and offers catharsis: we must first have Christianity in order to read Dante. Or as so accurately Chesterton observed: talking about Thomas Aquinas without referring to his religion is like talking about Antarctica without ever mentioning the snow. And who ever claimed that there is snow in Antarctica?

If I could merge two principles from the theory of photography: the *decisive* moment has to become, in collaboration with the reader, the *ongoing* moment. This is how the synergy between writers and readers is fulfilled. It is continuous because, every time someone reads a novel, they become one link in the chain of human curiosity and desire to become part of a never-ending story of things. This is what Bruce Chatwin discovered in Australia: the arcane symphonies that the landscape encoded, known to the inhabitants, but to which the new settlers were totally tone-deaf. Orhan Pamuk said of novelists: *From tiny experiences we build cathedrals*. In reality, the cathedrals are here before us, and these tiny experiences are catalysts which make them visible and transform them into the grand narratives of our insignificant life.

White knows that novelists cannot be ideologues. They must break down all generalisations and generalities. Herein lies the difference between Chekhov and Maxim Gorky. Chekhov, the doctor, knows that human life is about the vulnerability of the body, about sickness and pain. Gorky, the ideologue, idealises pain and suffering, using them for another story, which is not the story of the people who had those experiences. The same can be claimed about the very interesting but failed aesthetic projects of Sartre. From the pioneering *Nausea* (1938) to the futile, self-defeating project of *The Roads to Freedom* (1945-1949), Sartre confronted the limits of personal engagement – and that's why he struggled so persistently to discredit Freud. In an interview, he stated: "What is fundamentally false about a novel in which one constructs a character based on oneself is precisely that he is not *really* you. The differences you put into him, and which seem of no decisive significance at the outset, end up throwing him into falseness."

What saves a novelist from such falseness is irony, self-irony, indeed the systematic practice of self-distancing. Affectionate irony is White's emblematic narrative strategy, indeed his most persistent ethical stand, beyond the art of the novel. As Henri Matisse said: I do not paint things. I only paint the difference between things. The difference between characters makes White's prose prismatic and elusive, indeterminate and unpredictable. And we can add: so alien to the prevailing idols of today's writing tribes.

If novelists want to invent stories, they must always take a back step, suffusing their narrative with dramatic energy which cannot be predicated by the pragmatics or the veracities of the story's content. Like Proust's painting, the significance of the work is not in what is depicted but what is inferred through its structural configurations. In White, this accounts for the fact that, overall, we have no central characters in his books: the structure is based on linked episodes. One episode leads to the next, and another episode comes out of another episode.

Characters appear and disappear, and the writer is not particularly interested in depicting their destiny. Some critics accused White of not really loving his characters. This is the most interesting element of his mythopoeia. No sympathy or empathy: they appear in the story because they must destroy their myth. The myth remains inconclusive: the novel must never give unity to the contradictions of experience. Voss vanishes into thin air and no one cares for him, while Laura Trevelyan has a sore throat and must carry on with the life of a visionary spinster.

In a strange way, most of his novels are structured like the *Arabian Nights* or even Cervantes' *Don Quixote* (1615). In the fusion of both, which obviously created Rabelais and hence the European novel, structural continuity is held together by a special tone of voice: someone speaks while taking a step back, an attitude which indicates the beginning of European modernity inaugurated through Montaigne's ironic scepticism. Yet there is still a need for some thread to keep it all together. Irony is a novelist's principal defence mechanism for survival; it dominated the European novel until Romanticism, when novelists became advocates for a cause and discovered seriousness – or perhaps dullness.

In a way, White's novels take us back to Henry Fielding, Samuel Richardson, Daniel Defoe and Lawrence Sterne. They are in constant dialogue with Denis Diderot's *Jacques the Fatalist* (1780), Voltaire's *Candide* (1759) and Goethe's *Wilhelm Meister's Apprenticeship* (1796). They recapitulate the history of the genre all the way down to Dostoevsky, Proust, Joyce, Mahfouz, Godimer and Soyinka.

Meanwhile, all his characters are partners and collaborators in an invisible, transcendental transgression. They all have the propensity to be wrong; not simply to make mistakes and err, but to be ontologically in error. They know it – and this knowledge destroys them and liberates them simultaneously. In White's dark world of malefactors and reprobates, grace is found, indeed achieved, through the redeeming drudgery of a faithless existence.

After all, faith in any form of theodicy supposedly vanished with the Nietzschean death of God; and what else remained as the ultimate vestiges of the miraculous and the numinous in life, except the unwavering devotion to someone else's existence? The other incarnates the final frontier in metaphysics. Is there an end in this messy and disordered oscillation between illusions, distractions and evasions that could show how to arrive somewhere, or knock at someone's door? The might of illusion is invincible, the seduction of delusion uncontested. Only someone else can save you from the un-being of narcissism, the opaque inwardness of your own ego. What redemption can we have in a world without God? But didn't God withdraw somewhere in his garden alone, after the first humans could not look at him face to face?

We are left with that forlorn German professor, Nietzsche! He was the only true *dysangelist*. He never read the Bible. He always thought of his father and his Lutheran professors when he advertised his puerile metaphysics. What a pity also that, in his magnificent delusions about Greek tragedy, he never read Homer! The last rhapsody of *The Iliad*. The first rhapsody of *The Iliad*. Any rhapsody of *The Iliad*. He would have noticed that the real protagonist of this epic of war is the dead Hector, and that reconciliation and mercy were at the heart of the Greek miracle. And he never understood why Aeschylus wrote the earliest tragedy about the defeated Persians with the defeated Persians as protagonists, and not with the triumphant Greeks!

The difference between the Hellenic and the Germanic vision of the world. The German believed in *der Wille zur Macht*. The Greek talks about his opponent as his better, indeed as nobler than him. Because victory matters only when you overcome your superior, not when you destroy the one who is weaker than you. White knew that my power is perfected in weakness: because only when I am weak then am I strong – I have repeated this mantra several times in here. He linked himself with all those writers who explored weakness and dis-empowerment as the existential *urgrund* of human reality, Dostoevsky for example Proust, and Faulkner and Broch and Musil.

White's novels link themselves to the great novelistic tradition of collective redemption. Not to the ideas of possessive individualism that dominate the postwar Anglosphere, and especially the American book industry of false identifications. Now I know: Voss can never become a film hero: he is too unsettling and unsettled. Hurtle, too, but also Eddie/Eadith Twyborn, Waldo and Arthur Brown, Ellen Roxburgh, Mary Hare or Mordecai Himmelfarb, even Alf Dubbo: they are too confronting, too *immoral*, as characters, and cannot be reduced to the words that describe them in the novels.

A brief contrast between Mordecai Himmelfarb and Somerset W. Maugham's Larry Darrell in *The Razor's Edge* is enough to point out White's ability to avoid the simplistic pitfalls of individualism. In the end, Larry finds happiness thanks to the Bhagawan Ramana Maharshi; whereas Mordecai, after the experience of the Holocaust, becomes a humble clerk in a machine shop. Reality is always more illuminating than any otherworldly samsara. Readers, usually unprepared for reality in these days of emotional prolixity, feel intimidated and defeated by White's scope; and who can accept, in the era of self-admiring amateurism, that the book they read is much more complex than their own mind?

The question goes beyond what writing can do and why we write. It pertains to the foundational forms that arise from the chaos of the unconscious. "Do what you will, this Life's a Fiction / And is made up of contradiction," as William Blake stated. Such contradiction indicates our fundamental deracination from space and time: the sense of remoteness, of something beyond the horizon of our existence, which we will never see or touch. That's why my mind went to St Augustine, the jubilant poet of all unconsummated loves.

I keep returning to the final chapter of Stan Parker's silent Golgotha: *So that in the end there were the trees. The boy walking through them with his head drooping as he increased in stature. Putting out shoots of green thought. So that, in the end, there was no end.* When I re-read it recently, my involuntary memory jumped associatively over centuries and cultures and landed on the final paragraph of Augustine's *The City of God.* My beloved Latin brought me closer to reality again: *Ibi vacabimus, videbimus et amabimus, amabimus et laudabimus, Ecce quod erit in fine, sine fine.* "There, we shall be still and see, shall see and love, shall love and praise. Behold what shall be in the end, without end."

I felt fulfilled as a reader by the visions of the saint and the images of the novelist: all converging together, as the sum of all our fears and expectations, the peak moment which we experience once or twice and live afterward to reconstruct its power and magic. Language, the ultimate enemy, is conquered. Our final duty is silence, the consummation of all words. In the end, we are the end.

At a certain stage, we must acquire the intellectual honesty and moral courage to confront the unsolvable dilemmas of the human mind. The most beautiful world is like a heap of rubble tossed down in confusion, said Heraclitus. Within such rubble and confusion, we come to the horrible realisation that we are always *almost* there and will never finalise or complete anything. Our best works will never be written, our truest words will never be said.

Yet, we must overcome the fear of self-ridicule, or self-marginalisation, and proceed with the explicit formulation of the fundamentals that defined our journeys. This would bring us to the world without end. Grace and absolution come through another human. Closure comes through another human. Hope comes through another human. Not as an individual ascesis in virtue; or as the total deregulation of the senses; or as the complete immersion in the ecstasy of the absolute. You cannot enter paradise alone.

Patrick White's dilemmas found their resolution and culmination in Mr Manoly Lascaris – not in his novels. That's the paradox of all life: there must be a body on which the material and the symbolic converge. White's books were the commentaries to the great adventure that we see unfolding through their relationship. And its unfolding is firmly identified with that one person. *The purpose of my life was to find Manoly*, he wrote. What happened after he found him?

But I start from the end. What happened after I found him?

Enters Mr Manoly Lascaris

Mr Lascaris and I met in early January 1994. We became close for several years, then drifted apart. I think now that we always remained somehow suspicious of each other. We tried to connect through our common nostalgia and struggled to understand each other through White's writings. To no avail. Nothing was enough, or indeed mattered substantially to both of us at that stage of our existence. He was 84. I was not even 34. A huge chasm. Not simply a generational or personal gap: but a deep, cultural divide of different historical cycles.

He still lived in 1920; I was just discovering the fluidity of time. We spoke the same language which seemed enough – but it was not. We became distant because of our commonalities and lost the will to communicate because of everything we shared. Some phone calls now and then, for several years until his passing in 2003. All the fault was mine, of course. I was young and silly and hadn't realised that time never comes back. Everything in life is about unfinished friendships, incomplete encounters, or interrupted conversations. And, most frequently, as we reflect because we are the only ones left, we are to take the full blame. Our survival is our admission of guilt.

I wanted to know what White read. He wanted to talk about himself. He wanted to speak in his first language: "English, you know, shows only half of my face." At a restaurant once, he apostrophised in his elegant dialect: "Why isn't anyone asking: who are you, Mr Lascaris? What are you doing here? Why are you here? And," turning to me, "what about you, Mr *What's-Your-Name-Again*?" I didn't take the hint. I was absorbed by the translations. He looked around in despair and helplessness. I knew that look. I could recognise that gaze. It showed the face of the overlooked, the neglected, the disregarded. I encountered it in many people I knew, loved or unloved. On some occasions, it involved me and my presence in this colonial outpost. A face full of despair, anger and frustration or, possibly, resignation – yes, definitely, resignation.

Soon however, I started talking with him *about him*. For far too long, he had allowed the perception of an anti-intellectual, Sancho Panza myth to surround his name. Next to the great artist: a minor incident in his biography, a concession to the demands of life, White's butler and servant, as many journalists wrote. In an indirect way, by seeing how they lived, I thought that it will help me understand better the invisible conceptual undercurrents of the work. But in fact, it didn't. "Let the dead stay where they are," he said. In writing some recollections about him, I tried to exorcise his presence from my mind. But the devils are never cast out; they return demanding their place in the realm of the living, as long as time remains. Now that I am entering old age, I think that I can understand him better.

But I beg you read his books read his books you may find your best self in there you never know you may even imagine a better self because we all ignore our better self I can feel it and you are young and cannot see it but you know you never know something happens one day and the meaninglessness of existence becomes transparent and you don't know what to do if you know what I mean and you do nothing nothing you do because you are nothing and nothing begets nothing let me remind you that nothing begets nothing nothing all the rest is bad theology oh yes theology because theology is the ultimate temptation and the final destination the paternal absence that can never be healed in the world of dominant mothers but very few arrive there do you like Greek chocolate very few arrive at the final realisation do you like Greek chocolate I was never anything I was always nada nada a human absence I have some spare Greek chocolate if you like Mr What's-Your-Name-Again, I have lost my harbour and my essence my quintessence but you wouldn't know anything about this.

No pause to breathe in his endless and relentless diatribes against the rhythm of the world. Yet I insisted. Sometimes, even today, when I have grown old and clearly see the blurred colours of the horizon, I try to reconstruct and relive some of our discussions; 35 years later, under the heavy shadows of our dead friends, I only remember the quirky things he said about himself, his imperial family, his renegade mother, his lustful father, his sweet aunties, his sisters, his Athenian memories, his first lover, the great city of Alexandria, their experiences of the war, his departure from the first motherland, the day he arrived at Rose Bay in Sydney.

It was humid. I remember it well. It had rained the night before. New smells around me trees and flowers and birds. Where am I? I asked myself and bit my lips. Patrick was waiting for me with a new life. Am I dreaming? I thought. I should have died in Africa, in the Middle East. In the desert. I saw so much death you know. So many dying men. Patrick dragged me out of such darkness. Am I dreaming that I am still alive? Desire is death. Death is desire. Both were at the heart of our affair.

Some peculiar episodes remain in my memory: how he hummed the Greek national anthem. Or chanted *O my sweet Spring* from the lamentations of Good Friday. Or how he sang or tried to sing the rocking Misirlou, a song of Egypt, the eternal motherland of all storytellers. Through such snapshots, I could better understand his Australian life, indeed their Australian life as the inscape of love and fulfilment. He gave me his Ariadne's thread through the labyrinth of their common existence.

Labyrinth o yes that is the word the most important psychological symbol of antiquity it is not Ulysses' journey or Ithaca the ultimate symbol of meaning that we can take from antiquity no no no it's the labyrinth the endless and depthless dark caverns of the soul when you enter without assistance confronting the beast of your own character I was his labyrinth I gave him the line you are my desert *the ultimate phrase of his work we are somebody's desert at the end dream and nightmare the beauty they search for and the futility they feel after they got hold of you and you are always less than yourself you fall short of your existence and day after day you lose what makes you distinct and special and you become part of the house the atmosphere the garden if you know what I mean a nothing a nothing nada nada.* I wondered if he ever read Hemingway, which I truly think inconceivable.

I don't even know if Mr Lascaris ever read Manning Clark, who suggested that the central question of Australian experience is *the problem of the desert, the fatal flaw which leads a man or woman to destruction.* Through cryptic verbal ambiguities, he felt and expressed, in his own way, that in White's universe all characters are in no position to claim what they desire. They exist in a confusing void hovering over the possibilities of their strengths, which are also the causes of their demise.

He had a strange vision of Patrick's writing: *Yes, yes, we were each other's desert*, he said. He was himself a character from White's novels – or maybe White's novels were the manifestation of their common destiny? *Yes, yes, I was his desert.*

It took me decades to understand what he meant. Brave words by someone who never wrote anything, remaining silent and invisible. *My success in life*, White insisted, *is my discovery of Manoly. Nothing is of importance beside that. Books – shit!*

What can anyone add to that?

Exeunt Omnes

EPILEGOMENON

A Lost Letter to Patrick White

Dear Patrick,

We never met but I feel the obligation as reader of your books to introduce myself. Don't ask why. You have so many readers, many of whom are more eloquent and profound than the foreigner that is me. In fact, I had to translate into Greek two of your novels and one of your plays to understand you properly, to get under your skin. So, how can I explain myself? Sometimes I feel that my Mediterranean shallowness is the best way to enter your world. Sometimes, love for shiny surfaces goes deeper than the mysteries of split consciousness glorified by the demonic extravaganzas of your dark, telluric Protestantism. There is immense depth beneath all surfaces as Oscar Wilde said; it is confusing and liberating at the same time.

In a strange way, I knew your books before reading them – their stories, their characters, each scene, every episode, their style, their irregularities, their absurdities. They were inscribed in my mind although you wrote them before I was born in a place very far away. How paradoxical, so Platonic, really *unheimliche*. It sounds paranormal, I know, but this is how I felt. When I started reading them, I entered their flow without reservation or resistance. Theodora Goodman or Stan Parker or Hurtle Duffield or Miss Docker or Sir Basil Hunter – I knew that I had conversed with these voices in real life. They talked to me in my native tongue.

Reading is a pilgrimage; progress towards the retrieval of something lost, a home, which we probably never had, or a reconnection with a lost friend, through the recalling of a name. Our psyche loves long peregrinations.
It remains nomadic, a disorientated itinerant, even when we physically settle down for good, grow roots and stay motionless. Yet it still

searches for the impalpable substance of time that runs all the way through us, from the writing to the reading of every book. All your characters were around me: I had walked and talked with them as my mind was being formed. I had witnessed the architectural fatalities of their existence. I was a member of the various associations for the promotion of banality they advocated. I even knew the end of each one, if there is an actual end in them.

Such knowledge, premonition, intimation, call it what you like, prefigures the truth of unconscious communication that runs through our mind – pre-verbal, un-conceptualised, non-experiential, somehow almost unhistorical, pre-cognitive and eschatological, oftentimes abnormal and irregular, everywhere and for everyone, in all lands of the inhabited world.

Beyond the images, the episodes, the characters, the psychology, the ideology, the panic, the bliss, your sentences recorded a hyper-acoustic imagination I haven't heard before but in the grand symphonic poems of

John Milton. Music, yes, it is everywhere in your stories. It permeates your words.
It modulates your voice. Your word-music destroyed the marketing of the novel.
You never succumbed to the temptations of success. All because of music, the word-music, the liberation provoked only by spoken words: *Freedom. But prayer is freedom, or should be. If a man has got faith.* How can I get there when I have no faith? I read your books as incantations over mortality, as ritual re-enactments of lost affinities and bonds and recognitions.
They speak through what they do not declare.
They speak as intimations of things silenced before the act of writing was invented, of invisible things hoped for.

Where does their music come from? Is their sound a projection of our own mental chaos? Is music the crystallization of our inner void as silence is the offspring of the unspoken word? And then where are these sounds from? Are we echoing some tunes we heard when we were in our mother's arms? Or maybe, maybe, they were the vibrations permeating the amniotic fluids of the maternal cave before our birth when the brain's plasticity was absorbing everything and everything and everything? We shall never know, and we don't have to. The mystery of our consciousness is much more intriguing than all the answers we can give.

Can we distinguish the singer from the song? You and Milton, I know. Sometimes Dante, I know. Oh, yes, occasionally, Goethe, *Faust*, in German, certainly. You both sing of '*man's first disobedience and the fruit of the forbidden tree, whose mortal tast, brought death into the world and all our woe, with loss of Eden*... Or of the perpetual purgatory we all live in or of the daily selling out of our soul to the demons of insignificance. Or even closer to your heart: *Part of that force that always wills the evil and always produces the good.* This is how we all end up: to be unwillingly good – which is the real tragedy in a world which chooses to exist without destiny.

Anyhow, you know that no "greater man" could ever restore us, something that Milton suspected but didn't wish to confront. Like you, the Puritan poet liked parables; dark, demonic and didactic but also sardonic, playful and funny. How naïve, he was, how naïve we are, to think that in this endlessly expanding *multiverse* somebody cares for us, in our immense forlornness and narcissism. Stan Parker is all alone under the starry skies and on the barren land. How naïve to believe that a benevolent father created all this mess for him to find peace with his hidden presence in *a gobble of spit*.

The great magician Mordecai Himmelfarb never says anything about his traumatic time at the concentration camps. But, yes, we are indeed, so dangerously naïve, silly, silly.
We don't see because we know. *Illumination is synonymous with blindness*. In the end, after so many failures and horrible mistakes, we realise that there is no redemption, there is no redeemer, and we simply look around with love and disappointment before embarking to a metaphysical odyssey towards vague destinations. We take *the path of inwardness*, and

yet we are all lost. Only then we find our voice, the unique and unrepeatable vibrations that no one else could ever embody.

Meanwhile we are consumed by passions and obsessions that they don't give us the time to examine with kindness or good faith. Suddenly one day, we find ourselves in a strange place, in the land of lotus-eaters, and totally dazzled we look around with the feelings of mystical bewilderment found in the painting of Lascaux and Chauvet or the pictographs of Arnhem Land. *All truths are particoloured. Except the greatest truth of all,* because probably, instead of truths we are here to experience the natural ecstasy of being alive and paint it on rocks in secret caves, then seal the entrance and leave them in peace for thousands of years.

From the fragility of a great language, in its attempt to sing the guilt and the darkness of its beginnings in a new continent, you composed epic fables of premonition and prefiguration. From *Voss* to *A Fringe of Leaves* we see a whole society confronting its own deep truths: it questions its foundations without being afraid of the abyss' gaze. I particularly liked that there was no utopia or ideal city or restorative justice in your books. You accepted with humility the predicament of our body's history; fragile, vulnerable, helpless. You understood the primal crime that established this country. Your language exorcised its dark miasma.

Your writing was a Proustian texturing of the chronicles of human disintegration while struggling to imagine some characters, some names, to save the anxiety, the passion and the suffering, which destroyed all premonition of tranquillity, even momentarily in life. Like Kafka, however, you knew that literature is not about characters, but about symbols. Symbols mean eternity, they mean *attunement*: symbols intimate the absolute plenitude of nothingness, the place where there are no tensions or conflicts or collisions, the fertile nothingness of Zen Buddhism. Some of your pages are out of Dante's Paradiso; nothing happens in them, everything is flat, unemotional, unmoving – and yet full of life, colour, solidity. And the end is the ultimate beginning, the reason, the cause, the foundation: *l'amor che move il sole e l'altre stelle*. Do we need anything else?

In any case, I suspect that you knew: tranquillity, not happiness, ataraxia not contentment, is what we long for.

Some moments of equilibrium when everything flows around us noiselessly and seamlessly and we go along humming the songs of our childhood, in a dark forest, with many curious or voluptuous eyes looking at us while we can't even imagine their existence. After we are gone, someone will have the time and the imprudence to sit down trying to make sense of our chaotic existence and explore the thinkability of its symbols. Can we talk about vibrations, rhythms and echoes when we know nothing about their substance, their logos before becoming flesh?

This is what your books are: elegies and hymns, dedicated to the visible and invisible father, the sky, who begets time, who begets life, who begets language, who begets stories, who secures their truth, who redeems everything, who initiates everyone to the mysteries of form and disappears in pure transparency. You called it *permanence* in your best novel, the moment at the rose garden, the sublime moment of self-recognition – what we all long for but we are afraid to attain.

Pardon me, for a moment, I will be rather pedantic, one of those horrible academics you detested: your books existed in me as markers of a personal ontology of foundations. I never felt empowered by your stories. On the contrary, they disarmed me, they made me weak, feeble: I experienced my vulnerabilities through your books and their characters.

I regained my humanity through their cruelty. I was enraptured and terrified by their complexities, their cunning and uncanny reversals. You enabled me to avoid the normality of low expectations. In the end, I became stronger, unambiguous, calm—this is how it all ends. By reaching its own completion and culmination. Nowhere else to go after this: the triumphant cry *Consummatum est* can be proclaimed. Death has won. It always wins. But we exist because of our birth and not for our death. The mystery of being born innocent and doomed, that is the key to your secret garden, as the two kids in your last and unfinished novel indicate. But which writer was ever able to depict innocence, in lives that are full of fault and blame?

Many think that novels are written to educate, guide, entertain, instruct, or persuade. You have always known that we write stories to foreground the numberless fragments that our everyday life is made of. Nothing can unify them: neither ideology, nor belief, neither aesthetics, nor ethics. Novels capture the hidden workings of names and the magic of words, those primordial influences that exist beyond everything written or said. You name something and thus you control it: it's an old trick. The Egyptians had it and the Babylonians had it, even the Neanderthals probably had it:

by naming all nameable presences we control our fears, our demons, our death. We exorcise demons only if we know their name. But the twist comes here: the names that exorcise become the names that take possession of our mind and become our idols.

You avoided the allure of abstractions and gave your readers a compendium of fascinating names: Hurtle Duffield is my favourite. But also, Ulrich Voss, Laura Trevelyan, Mordecai Himmelfarb, Theodora Goodman and of course the grandest and most invisible character throughout your work, Mr Manoly Lascaris – too real and pragmatic to be addressed here in fictional or meta-fictional terms. Or, ultimately, that incredibly flawed character called Patrick White whom you lured out of Mr Lascaris' unconscious, added it to the front cover of your books and presented in such an abysmally erratic manner. You should have worked more meticulously on him. He really needed more attention, more care, more love, whatever they call it these days.

In your stories, I felt that things were beyond my control and made me the weakest link in the chain of beings. The narcissistic proclivity of modern writers to flatter our ideas and present aspects of our existence as inevitable moments of social reality was gratefully absent from your books. Your ideal fellow countryman, Gustav Flaubert, said that every generation wants its writers to flatter its own illusions –and you would have none of that. But then, books which do not flatter their readers? Who wants to read and buy them?

Most contemporary writers love to idolize gender, identity, sex, race and whatever the media finds useful in distracting us from the fundamental questions of existence. The Booker Prize was awarded to J.G Farrell's *Troubles* but not to *The Vivisector*. Years after their publication and after most of their contemporaries are gone, books become symbolic maps over the complex web of interests, frustrations and delusions that determined their reception. *The Vivisector* remains next to Goethe's *Wilhelm Meister*, Flaubert's *Madame Bovary*, Dostoevsky's *The Underground*, Zola's *The Masterpiece*, Thomas Mann's *Doctor Faustus*, Marguerite Yourcenar's *The Abyss*; Farrell's trilogy and almost all the Booker Prize recipients have been totally forgotten and nobody has any curiosity to search for them.

But what is the difference? The foundational difference, I mean. After having read almost all history books on Australia, from all sides of the spectrum, I didn't learn anything about the Australians themselves. I was still an onlooker. I was an intruder, an alien; and these books didn't help me to become part of the society I was living in. They told me little about the people or the place. Nothing about their inner dilemmas, their dreams, nightmares, convulsions of regret, elations of joy. Who were those notorious monsters who conquered the land, exterminated the indigenous people, destroyed the green pastures, persecuted the immigrants and established "the lucky country" which only they themselves had the right to enjoy? What did they feel? How do they see themselves today? Is there any remorse? Any repentance? Admission of guilt? Any self-irony?

Is there any redeeming element in them that would allow us to look into their psyche and see the quivering, scared and crucified conscience that might free and rebaptise them? That will make them admit their self-betrayal and make amends? And what about those who were decimated, by disease and extermination, perished unrecorded by administrative archives? Did these authors ever ask them who they were? What they believed in or how they buried their dead? Did they ever notice the invisible geographies that hover over the natural landscape, which the newcomers judged empty, while its inhabitants knew that it was pulsating with life and spirits and genealogies?

You are the only historian of human emotions in this colonial outpost – and remain so to this day. When I want to understand how people come together and fall apart in this land, I read your *Tree of Man* and *A Fringe of Leaves*: they record patterns of sociability and forms of expression so clearly and vividly that you feel they were written for today. They give you the ruler to measure aptitudes and attitudes: what you can accept, what you must reject, how you can contribute. On the contrary, when I read lengthy books by famous, award-winning historians, sociologists or glorious journalists, I learn nothing about the living or the dead while I learn about the methods each one of them employed to explain the past or control the present. Can human experience fit into a method?

You did what you did because you knew the subtle difference between plot and story. You worked to disentangle them. Plotless stories in the Anglosphere? Who wants to commit such blasphemy? But you were relentless. You knew that reality is not a personal invention, a narrative that we concoct to avoid the rough edges of everydayness. Reality is waiting for us, cruel, indifferent, and carnivorous. We learn about reality day by day and yet it remains inexhaustible. The only infinity we can enjoy is in thinking of the many humans who exist and the fact that we will never know them, or them know us. Our mind is always more than the total sum of our thoughts. Our thinking is always more that we could ever conceptualise.

Therein lies the difference between your work and that of E.M. Forster, Joseph Conrad, Thomas Mann, William Golding, J.M. Coetzee, W.G. Sebald or Iris Murdoch. The space between Flaubert and Hemingway is truly a harsh terrain of improbabilities. There is the icy territory established by the forgotten greats of the north – Selma Lagerlöf and Knut Hamsun and Pär Lagerkvist – but who wants to enter that world? And between Tolstoy and Dostoevsky, therein lives only a vast desert of religious fantasies. But from Muriel Spark to Margaret Atwood and from V.S Naipaul to John Banville, Peter Carey to Helen Garner is nothing more than the safe re-elaboration of journalistic prosaisms. Too much realism ends in journalism. Because you knew the abyss that separates Hemingway from Hunter S. Thompson, you populated the Australian desert with improbabilities, with stories within stories, with stories unheard of before you, before the fatal day of the First Fleet, before all sense of conscious existence, as if you were falling falling falling into the abyss of preverbal beingness. Art is the weightlessness of existence: you fail and yet fly. The happy failure as they used to say. You know that everything excessive is discarded and what is absolutely natural drives you upwards towards *Das Unzulängliche*, the undeclarable, the indescribable, the unverbalizable as explored by the great devourer of words, Rainer Maria Rilke.

But you had to offer your testimony and it was truly hard. You tried to imagine the mythopoetics that localise finitude and ephemerality. Not like the florid postmodern gardens of Vladimir Nabokov or the Asiatic prose of Thomas Wolfe, or the fabulistic world of Gabriel García Marquez. Rather, you did this through your dissociative prose, the articulation of disjunctions, which made reading more confusing and complex and perhaps distressing. *We all desire to be seen as we are not*. To become the idealised subject matter of somebody else's gaze. To vanish as individuals and re-emerge as immaculate *imago* in someone else's mind. From everyday types we want to become perennial archetypes; and why not? Is there something missing in us? Yet you knew Goethe all too well: We are all Fausts in the end, seduced and betrayed, singing prayers to the innocence of our youth, lost now and half-remembered but always misunderstood.

How can we confront the face under the mask when we cannot distinguish between them anymore? We all afraid to confront the ultimate concern: we can never know who we are. What we will know will be misleading; what we will gain will be our loss.

Absolution comes through self-othering: if you don't surrender yourself to somebody else's gaze, you can never say *I am who I am*. Even if we envision and dream of the face-to-face encounter with aliens, the chariots of fire, there will always be in us the endless and tragic curiosity to see, touch, taste and admire what is not us, what will never be, what will always transcend and transform us into eternal children, parentless and rootless, full of confusion and sadness and expectation. Like the transfigured body of Jesus after the resurrection, waiting somewhere for… what? Yes, what?

It is obvious that you detested your enslavement to language. Samuel Beckett knew this feeling also, somehow indirectly. He was taking energy out of Marcel Proust and, since therein was life abundant, his work sparkles with the impossibility, the infeasibility, of writing. This brought him closer to your negativity: I exist therefore I am negated. Your prose negated the possibility of its own writing

– yet the paradox of writing is that it cannot annul its own actuality. It is too Aristotelian, I know. The *ergon* exists only as energeia: through writing, writing becomes possible. But let me stop here and you ignore my clumsy philosophising.

The novel was never meant to be anything beyond entertainment by the fireplace. Then Cervantes came and then Rabelais and then Lawrence Stern and things moved away from the hearth, and we all fell into the liberating condition of sinfulness, being miserable and majestic at the same time as Pascal thought, *simul justus et peccatus*, as Martin Luther declared. You made your outcasts to be the psychopomps to the paradoxical realm of human interiority.

Today, in the times of emotional puritanism and sentimental incontinence, novels have no role to play beyond that of keeping company during long flights and early morning trips when the internet is not available, by singularising what we are. The old blurred convex has become the smooth mirror of all vanities. Yet, on occasion, it still shakes and disturbs and disrupts, it brings back the memory of forgotten moments and places, it revives the innocence of childhood and the wonderment in the eyes of people who have been consumed by suspicion and distrust and nothingness. History comes in us through a perpetual loss of innocence: and after we lose it all, only then we become historical. In your world, even evil has the right to exist, if of course evil really exists and is not simply the consequence of our unwillingness to communicate with each other.

Everything has its place in your scheme of things: you avoided completely the murky puritanism of the British novel. The multiplicity of beings means that everything has the right to exist. It reflects what a Byzantine mystic said, that if the mystery of the Divine is ineffable, there is no space for heresies in theology. Or as Master Kakuzo Okakura observed, 'in religion the Future is behind us. In art the Present is the eternal." Everything is one, yes, or as you stated in your credo because of *these humble everyday saints created for our consolation by the same mysterious universal Presence, ignored, cursed, derided, or intermittently worshipped by the human race.* There is no *there* in your works: only here and nothing else.

I read your novels in their absolute *otherness* and difference from what I like or even what I accept as literary. I don't like projecting on their structures what is in me and what I want to find to confirm the validity of my insights. Contemporary readers tend to try to detect copies of their own ideas, preferences or inclinations; this superstitious cult of unhinged *presentism,* which leads to the idea that everything in the past must be judged and appreciated by our current concerns, is historically asymmetrical and morally objectionable.

I read your books again and again and I read about your books again and again. All I want is to locate the centers of your aesthetic and moral universe, the points that cannot be reduced to the specificities of your times or the expectations of your era. Who expected Stan Parker when he appeared? Only when we locate the irreducible elements of language, are able to read novels, indeed all novels, as imaginative constructions of self-recognition and not as journalistic documentations of an era's panics. The moment I recognise something of myself in a novel, I know for sure that there is something wrong with the novel or with me. Novelists show us what we would be unable to discover by ourselves. They announce the new birth within the real, the sudden embodiment of our expectations.

In an era of gnostic cults, orthodoxy dictates that novels, poems or essays are written through the colour of your skin, the whims of your desires or the privileges of your race. The Manicheans and the zealots have taken power and they are having serious fun. Savonarola's Florence and Calvin's Geneva are now the model-cities for our highly praised, and priced, identities. How can anyone enjoy Homer or Shakespeare if they grow up with such aesthetic formlessness? Where is Shakespeare you will ask? Who could write Shakespeare? Why are we so terrified by the simplest of his lines? My gaze was hovering over your pages one night. I found myself again in *the opalescent shallows of childhood* and your sentence was what I needed to keep myself strong and in one piece in the deserts of the mind and the dark oceans of reality.

Once again forgive my ranting. Inevitable to those who love. Forgive also my politicising. Politics are dead today although politicians thrive and rule. The visions of a big society have become the hallucinations of tribal communities, which inevitably one day will turn against each other. Alaric is in the City, and we pay no attention to the imminent dominance of oblivion.

The culture of waste has always existed, ever since our forefathers were expelled from paradise. We know unfortunately that our punishment is greater than what we can bear. I am used to it. I have internalised it. It is part of me. As it was part of you. Your works embody the conscience of unbearable honesty, about *what you do not know but know*, which is absent from the eternal nows that constitute our post-this-and-post-that subjectivities. Today, we are mandated to celebrate the fragmented moments that give voice to the cheerful psychopaths we all are.

You resisted all that. What would Cervantes say about you? Or Rabelais. Or Jonathan Swift, Goethe, or Lawrence Sterne. They are your lot. You are not alone. There is also Wagner, there is Liszt, Mendelssohn and Brahms. Your guiding angels. Your beloved Germans. No Plato or other Greeks, save one. I am sorry for talking so much. Recently I started sending letters to old friends and distant intellectual companions, in many forms and languages. But dare I say, please don't misconstrue my prolixity. It is the offspring of solitude, of the immense void left behind after the horrible encounter with *Das Es* – and you know what I mean.

Finally, something truly important: how is Mr. Lascaris these days? I miss him terribly. We parted abruptly and on somewhat bad terms. Please do tell him that I found the word he was looking for in his beloved Byzantine dictionary. We quarrelled for days. We had the notion but not the word. That dictionary was the undoing of our friendship. Finally, now, so many years later, I found the word suddenly without even looking for it. It was a word within a word, quite tricky. As he knows quite well, we have been trapped by the Byzantines to this day. They knew how to turn meanings, inwards. They were mischievous *inverterians*, as he used to say. He may decide to reveal the word to you. Just say, the Greek friend found the word. He will understand.

As ever, waiting for news and, if possible, for a meeting, sometime soon.

VK

ABOUT THE AUTHOR

VRASIDAS KARALIS holds the Chair of Sir Nicholas Laurantos in Modern Greek and Byzantine Studies at the University of Sydney. His main areas of research are Greek studies, Film Studies, Greek-Australian Literature, Byzantine Culture and Theology, and the work of Patrick White. His main publications in English include, *A History of Greek Cinema* (Continuum 2012), *Realism in Greek Cinema* (I.B. Tauris 2017), *The Cinematic Language of Theo Angelopoulos* (Berhghan Press 2021), *Theo Angelopoulos: Filmmaker and Philosopher* (Palgrave 2023), *Recollections of Mr Manoly Lascaris* (Brandl & Schlesinger 2007), *The Demons of Athens* (Brandl & Schlesinger 2013), *Reflections on Presence* (re.Press 2016) and *The Glebe Point Road Blues* (Brandl & Schlesinger 2021). His personal memoir *Farewell to Robert* (Brandl & Schlesinger 2023) has been translated into Greek and nominated for best translation state awards.

He has edited volumes on Martin Heidegger, Hannah Arendt and Cornelius Castoriadis. He has been the President of the Modern Greek Studies Association of Australian and New Zealand. He is the editor of *Modern Greek Studies* (Australian and New Zealand) and on the board of a number of academic and literary journals. He is currently working on a book length study on the concept of the sublime as expressed and visualised in contemporary cinema.

In Greek his publications are varied and diverse. He has translated four volumes of Byzantine historiography, and has written monographs on Nikos Kazantzakis, Dionysios Solomos and Andreas Angelakis. His recent memoir *The Stories of my Grandmother* (Doma 2024) has become a best-seller. He has received the prize of the Greek Translators League for his translation of Patrick White's *Voss*. He received the highest honour awarded to a lay person by the Patriarch of Constantinople, who gave him the title of the Ecumenical Archon of the Word. He has translated Patrick White's *Voss* and *The Vivisector*, as well as well Michael Dransfield's and Martin Johnston's poems into Greek.

Vrasidas Karalis was elected Fellow in the Australian Academy for the Humanities in Canberra.